Bill Clark is not only a world [barcode obscures text] *...ber of the Strength and Power H* [barcode] *...nd. Every sport has its stars, and Bill is one of the greats in the strength world. Several years ago, I was able to watch Bill compete in the Buffalo, NY area. In addition to his obvious strength and power, what caught my attention the most was his incredible intensity. One minute, he would be smiling and talking to the other lifters back in the warmup area, and then, almost with the snap of a finger, he transformed into a different person; fearless, like a soldier that focused solely on what he was told to do. He'd become very quiet, his facial expressions would change, he would even walk differently, and then on to the platform he would step. He looked like he was on a search and destroy mission, and he was. Bill even intimidated the audience. But as soon as the lift was over, he was right back to his happy, kind, and loving self, answering questions from people, and talking with everyone that approached him. I think that is one of the things that makes Bill's part of the book so special. The reader is almost getting a hands-on tutorial of not only what's possible when you put your mind to it, but how to do it too. I could go on and on about my buddy Bill, but it's probably best that you read his words for yourself. One thing further I can tell you about Bill is that he cares about people. He is a Christian brother, who puts others before himself, and he has done that with his book as well. Happy Reading!*

—Don Reinhoudt
5 Time Winner of The World's Strongest Man
Multiple World Powerlifting Champion
World Record Holder
Motivational Speaker and Professional Strongman
Director of Chatagua County Youth Bureau
Strength and Power Hall of Fame Inductee

I have known Trent since he was an 18 year old high school senior. We were in the same class at Alabama. Not only were we teammates, we played next to each other for 4 years and our lockers were next to each other too. When it came time for me to choose a teammate to be on the "Biggest Loser Couples," my first call was to Trent. Trent is a great role model and I knew when we were on the "Biggest Loser," he would be there to motivate me and also show me the way. Trent lives what he teaches and that's why he has had a big impact on the people he coaches in the weight room, football field and in life. If you are looking for a resource that can motivate you, I would recommend this book. As a matter of fact, I would recommend you purchase a bunch and give them as gifts.

—ROGER SHULTZ
4-year starter 2 time All - SEC Center at the University of Alabama
Runner up on the Biggest Loser, season 5
Radio personality

Anyone wanting to become a champion athlete, or for that matter a 'Champion' in any field of endeavor would best be served by reading Bill Clark's book, "LIFTING SPIRITS." Having known Bill since he was a 12 year-old, shy, introverted, insecure boy & seeing him develop into a World Champion athlete & world class motivational speaker & 'word smith' has been one of the greatest joys of my life! Known as the "Humble Warrior" and a "Champion's Champion," Bill will take you on an inspirational journey on how he took personal adversity and turned it around, with the help of many others, into a life full of accolades, world record accomplishments & much more. Bill Clark has truly become a success, by any measure, in every facet of his life! Bill's goal in this book is to educate & demonstrate how YOU can become a CHAMPION in your chosen arena(s)!

—Larry Bucchioni
28-time World Champion Drug Free Powerlifter
Strength and Power Hall of Fame Inductee
Motivational Speaker
Teacher

Trent has the perfect combination of heart and hustle in all aspects of life. His passion and drive create the perfect storm to help elevate your game both mentally and physically. Trent's aura is something you definitely will want to be part of. To teach and coach with such belief and passion is truly a gift that Trent possesses. Trent and "lifting Spirits" will keep you 110% engaged for your ultimate success in life. "Lifting Spirts" will become your go to #1 resource to motivate, encourage and inspire you when you need a quick pick me up reminder!

—Debra Walter
Strategic Account Executive

LIFTING SPIRITS

WORLD CHAMPION ADVICE FOR EVERYDAY LIVING

BILL CLARK AND TRENT PATTERSON

BALBOA.
PRESS

A DIVISION OF HAY HOUSE

Copyright © 2017 Bill Clark & Trent Patterson.

Jennica Crissman: Created the title name of the book.
Jeffrey Rice: Created the conceptual art for the cover.

All rights reserved. No part of this book may be used or reproduced by any means, graphic, electronic, or mechanical, including photocopying, recording, taping or by any information storage retrieval system without the written permission of the author except in the case of brief quotations embodied in critical articles and reviews.

Balboa Press books may be ordered through booksellers or by contacting:

Balboa Press
A Division of Hay House
1663 Liberty Drive
Bloomington, IN 47403
www.balboapress.com
1 (877) 407-4847

Because of the dynamic nature of the Internet, any web addresses or links contained in this book may have changed since publication and may no longer be valid. The views expressed in this work are solely those of the author and do not necessarily reflect the views of the publisher, and the publisher hereby disclaims any responsibility for them.

The author of this book does not dispense medical advice or prescribe the use of any technique as a form of treatment for physical, emotional, or medical problems without the advice of a physician, either directly or indirectly. The intent of the author is only to offer information of a general nature to help you in your quest for emotional and spiritual well-being. In the event you use any of the information in this book for yourself, which is your constitutional right, the author and the publisher assume no responsibility for your actions.

Any people depicted in stock imagery provided by Thinkstock are models, and such images are being used for illustrative purposes only.
Certain stock imagery © Thinkstock.

Print information available on the last page.

ISBN: 978-1-5043-9174-0 (sc)
ISBN: 978-1-5043-9175-7 (hc)
ISBN: 978-1-5043-9201-3 (e)

Library of Congress Control Number: 2017917275

Balboa Press rev. date: 05/10/2018

DEDICATIONS

Bill Clark: First and foremost, I want to thank Jesus Christ! You guided me when no one else could. Thank you for making the events of my life possible. To my Mom and Dad: Thank you for everything. My Dad bought me my first weight set when I was in the second grade. He must have known something. My mom, when I was in high school, used to get up at 5 in the morning to drive me to the gym for my first training session of the day. Thank you for everything in between, as well. A special thanks to my sponsors who paid my expenses, and to Kathy Rader for helping to edit! To my incredible coaches who taught me so much more than just how to lift weights. To all of my relatives and friends, many of which are brothers and sisters: Thank you for your support, guidance, and faith. Thank you to the world's strongest men, Don Reinhoudt and Larry Bucchioni for writing the back cover of the hard-bound edition. To my wife and children: To try and put down in words what you have done and meant to me is to minimize your contributions, so I will simply say, " I love you!" With people like this in my life, I couldn't possibly lose. It is with beyond measure that I say, "I love and thank you all!"

Trent Patterson: To my loving Mom and Dad: Thank you for all of the encouragement, knowledge and motivation you have given me over the years and showing me the true meaning of unconditional love. To my mother in law, sister in law, sister, nephews, nieces, aunts, uncles, cousins and anyone I've ever called a "friend," thank you for being there for me and supporting me thru all of my endeavors and different stages in life and allowing me to lean on you from time to time. To my "Bama" family, coaches, teammates, Alumni (past and present), training staff, equipment staff, professors and fans, thank you for making my dreams of being a part of and contributing to that rich Alabama football tradition come true! My whole experience at the Capstone was truly amazing! And, to Shel, the love of my life, and my two handsome sons Linc & Mack, thank you for your unconditional love and patience as I completed this undertaking. Thank you for believing in me. You mean the world to me & I Love You!

CONTENTS

PART I: *In the Beginning*

PART II: *Paving Your Path to Victory*

PART III: *Paying it Forward*

PREFACE AND ABOUT THE COVER

On a snowy January day in 2016, I was at my doctor's office discussing the future of my lifting career. I had recently injured my neck while bending a ¾ inch steel bar over my head at one of my motivation presentations. As we talked, my doc said to me, "Bill, I'm worried about you." I'm worried that the next time you get hurt it won't be as easy to fix. You're the kind of guy that when he sets his mind to something, it gets done. I think you should retire from competition and write a book!"

Later that night, I called two former coaches that I knew I could trust, Larry Bucchioni and Don Reinhoudt. Both thought it would be a great idea, and Larry continued further by telling me that it was probably more than ½ way done because of my motivational speaking. I just needed to put my voice into the written word. I went right to work that night, putting my thoughts down on paper. For me, writing is easier than talking, and that is why I was able to write about some things that I was never able to talk about publicly before, such as the death of my dad. Quite honestly, I found the process to be very therapeutic. The other day I was interviewed by several students involved in a sports trainer program from a college about an hour away, and I was able to discuss my father without choking up, and that was a first. When you get to reading that chapter, the associated difficulties will become much clearer to you, and I think you'll understand why it had been so hard to talk about.

A couple of months went by and I continued to work away at the completion of the book. Up until the month of April (2016), this was a solo project. I was walking down the hallway at work with my good friend and co-author Trent Patterson when the book subject came up. Trent and I already have a personal security business together, so when the book came up in our conversation, it didn't take much for the individual project to morph into a team one. I'm glad too, because Trent is the kind of friend who will stand right beside you when the difficulties of life, or writing, hit their hardest.

We put together a plan to blend our respective messages, and started getting down to business. As the weeks went by, the book's concepts began to take shape and the stories began to breathe the air of life. Weeks turned into months and completion was ever so close. What we didn't know however, was that writing the book was only half the battle. Appeasing the evaluators and the lawyers was a much more difficult process. Permission had to be gained from everyone mentioned and involved, and in some cases, if permission was not attainable, names and places had to be changed. Hours and hours were spent on the phone with publishing agents and personnel. Almost as much time was spent solving political and legal problems as was spent writing. We can honestly state that writing this book was one of our biggest challenges, but we're glad we took it on. As the saying goes, it's a long and hard climb to the top of the mountain, but the view is awesome. Please enjoy reading this. Take your time, get out a pen, and make notes throughout the pages and chapters. Hopefully, our real-life stories and experiences will resonate with you in such a way as to put you into the proper frame of mind to attack your goals with the determination of the champion that you have the potential to be. Big things usually come from small steps taken, and the sooner you get moving, the quicker you can reach your dreams. Go get after it!

Finally, we would like to thank Jennica Crissman and Jeffery Rice for their contributions to this book. Trent and I were struggling to come up with a title for this book. We found that to be just as challenging as the development of the content. After continuing the fight for several weeks, I decided to share the situation with my students, some of which are incredibly gifted. Almost immediately after requesting help, Jennica Crissman suggested, "Why don't you call it, *Lifting Spirits*?" Even though I was already sold on the title, she continued, "You know, because you're a world record holder and strongman, and you're helping people out. Do you get the connections?" I called Trent on the phone and ran it by him. He was just as thrilled with it as I was, but it didn't come from us. It was Jennica's idea, and we want everyone to know it!

The cover art was originally designed by Jeffery Rice, another highly talented student from one of my classes. Writing a book is no easy task, and getting everyone to agree on its details is no less daunting. Trent and I were sold on the ideas that Jeffery had put forward, but again, it's hard to get everyone on, please excuse the play on words, the same page (I know-that's really bad). Unquestionably, Mr. Jeffery Rice has a brilliant future ahead as both an artist, and as a man!

Once again, Trent and I would like to thank both Jennica Crissman and Jeffery Rice for their contributions to this book. Both have great days ahead and we are honored to have been able to see a small part of their talents at work.

To all of our readers: Have fun!

INTRODUCTION

The purpose of this book is to share our knowledge as former elite level athletes, professionals in the working world, coaches, and members of the team called humanity in such a way as to help propel you to the mountain tops of your dreams. I use the word team because we are all members of the same fraternity, connected in so many fashions and ways, and I think that should be a source of comfort. All of us share the same emotions, fears, concerns, and desires. We feel happy when good things come our way, and not so much when the storms of life hit us hard. Although much of the contents included herein are our reflections on life, this work is by no means an autobiography, and should never be mistaken as such. This book is about you!

Our collective goal is to pass along lessons learned and provide you with the necessary fuel to reach your highest of aspirations. We hope and pray that as you read our stories, you will get a sense of encouragement, a sense of determination, and an overall feeling that it is possible to become something that you, up until now, never dreamed of. As you make your way through the pages that detail certain aspects of our lives, our wish is that you will feel as though we are right there beside you, cheering you on! Trent and I believe in the human spirit and that everyone possesses talents unique to themselves. Your challenge is to find them, develop and cultivate them, and turn these things into a product that you will be proud of.

Of course, this is a process and success to any great level won't come easily, but we think that it is well worth the sacrifices and prices paid. In large part and when you see superstars in any area of life, you are viewing a completed product. That's important to remember, because when you begin comparing yourself to others you often feel as though you don't rate, as though you are inferior, and that is simply not true. You are on your own unique course and path. You are your own person, capable of so much, and that is regardless of what others do or don't do.

The chapters you are about to read will also take you on our journey, one that we hope will inspire you. As such, the book is divided into sections or parts. We have included stories from our developmental days in grade school, as athletes, and then as retired athletes now passing knowledge on to anyone willing to listen. Whether we are writing about the Olympic Training Center, the philosophy of the University of Alabama football program, weightlifting adventures in different countries, or battles on the one-yard line, we believe that our experiences can help to jump-start you on your road to success. We genuinely want to thank you for reading our stories, and for including us on your team. We are both proud and happy to be a part of it too. Finally, we wish you the ultimate in success, health, happiness, and love. God bless and happy reading!

Affirmations:

1) Today I will recognize my own potential, and pursue those things that I have a love for.
2) Today I will start a new course for my life.
3) Today I will begin to see the world in a new and exciting way.

DISCLAIMER

Even though we probably don't know you personally, we care! We believe that our experiences can help you to live a better and more productive life, but our experiences are just that, experiences. We are not psychologists or medical doctors of any kind. We have worked extensively with both, but that does not qualify us to diagnose or treat any condition. Before you take up an exercise routine or if you are struggling with anxiety, depression, or anything of the like, please see a health care professional. There is always a solution to your problems, and unless otherwise prescribed by your MD, it never comes in the form of a needle, bottle, or from someone selling substances on the corner of the street. In fact and if you choose to travel down that path, you will find that you have effectively multiplied your problems. Be strong and defeat those temptations. Please believe us when we tell you that there is no shame in seeking help. The real shame is knowing that there is a problem, realizing that help is available, and still refusing to take it. Again, we care about you! We consider you part of our extended and larger team, so please do what is needed to be at your very best. In this book, we share many of our life's episodes and the advice that has been given to us, but again, we are not doctors. We are only able to pass along what has worked for us in the past, and that does not necessarily mean that it will work for you. Consider what we have said and then decide on your own merit whether or not to implement our ways of living. It is with all sincerity that we thank you for reading *Lifting Spirits: World Champion Advice for Everyday Living.* We wish you the very best in everything that you do, and hope that one day our paths can cross in person!

Affirmations:

1) Today I will take the necessary steps to get my life in order. I will see my health care professional and get cleared to start my journey of physical, mental, emotional, and spiritual fitness.

2) Today I will corral and take control of all the negative thoughts that used to pull me off of my path to success.

3) Today, and forever more, I will reject those lifestyle choices that put me into a negative state of mind, or worse. Today, I choose the victorious life!

PART ONE

In the Beginning

I know it's a cliché and it's probably not the first time you've heard this, but "Champions are never born, they are built." Some may be more advantaged than others, but hard work and years of dedication to a cause is always necessary if the highest of prizes are to be won. Our backgrounds certainly weren't privileged, but strangely enough, we found that the difficulties of our youths served not as curses, but as blessings. Those tough days taught us values that many of our peers never learned, and that set us apart. We learned at very young ages to endure and overcome. We learned to focus on things beyond that of our present circumstances, and again, that made us comparably unique. It allowed us to have a competitive dimension that years down the road would serve us very well. In this section, we include a number of chapters about our younger days that we believe can be of help to people of all ages. From the death of my father and how that set a new course for my life, to Trent's upbringing in Syracuse, NY and his life-altering choice to become a division one football player, we explain how to handle difficult times and turn them into opportunities.

No one can control all of the variables of life, but we can certainly control how we respond to them. For the record, and as I explain later, there is a fundamental and glaring difference between reaction and response. Included in these chapters is advice on how to do exactly that, to develop a proper and well executed response. We hope that this, in and of itself, will go a long way in the pursuit of becoming the best that you can be. Our examples illustrate how to build a plan of action and set a course for life, how to handle adversity, and just as importantly, how to stay focused on your goals and dreams even when it appears that they are stepping further and further out of reach.

Deeper still, lives are similar to houses. For both to be effective, there must be a strong and solid foundation, and that starts at the beginning. I have heard it said before that it is never too late to begin again, and we believe that is true. Whether you are 15 or 65, you can start a new life, and it can begin as soon as now. Our hope is that every pain and hardship that we have endured will serve as a source of motivation and strength for you. Even though we may never get the opportunity to meet you in person, and we honestly hope that we do, we want you to know that we are supporting you in every way feasible. We want you to succeed, and we know that it is possible for you to do so. Your new life begins today! Live it with the very best of every intention, with love, strength, and a total commitment to a better you!

Affirmations:

1) Today I will show my true spirit of strength and kindness to people.
2) Today I choose not to allow people on a path of opposition to put me into a state of mind that I don't care to have.
3) Today I will choose to use the difficult experiences of the past for my benefit.

CHAPTER 1

Failure Turned Inside Out

This is the only picture that we have as a family. Two better parents never existed!

Hidden in the pain and turmoil of failure lies great opportunity, but we have to search for it. Searching is a verb, and that means that it takes action, so you won't find it by complaining about what went wrong or by stewing over what could have been. I am not trying to be insensitive here because I also know the sorrow that comes with life. However, it is possible to overcome and learn from the difficult and even painful circumstances of what has been dealt to you. We aren't always able to control the things that happen to us, but we do get to choose our response to them. Failure is often embedded in those difficult situations and has the potential to be life changing, either negatively or positively. My biggest failure came when I was in the 7th grade, and it impacted me more than almost any other event in my life.

My mom and dad had separated, and my father was living in an apartment on the south side of town. Despite their separation, both instilled within me a love for God and codes of behavior and honor that

I still try to follow to this day. Simply stated, my parents were awesome! However, we all have our vulnerabilities, and there are things beyond which we can handle alone. The Lord knows how hard living can be, and my parents fought with serious life-changing, and in some cases, life-taking issues. As you may have already figured, my dad's health was failing, and quickly so. At that stage of their relationship, my mother and father were oppositional, and when they did see each other, which they both tried to avoid, it wasn't a visit of warmth and/or comfort. One day, my dad called and told me to come over to his apartment, as he had something that he needed to give to me. Several hours later, I entered my father's apartment, and saw him looking weaker than I had ever seen anyone, but I failed to recognize its severity. Maybe it was denial on my part; I just don't know. What I do know is that I could have handled the situation much better, and unfortunately, it was about to get exponentially worse.

My dad, trying to maintain his physical stability but stumbling around his kitchen, handed me a check for a small amount of money. I didn't know it at the time, but he was emptying out his bank account. He also shared a few very deep and personal stories which was quite a stretch from his ordinary character. My dad was dying, and he knew it. He never shared that with me, but any idiot could have recognized it. Any idiot except me, that is. My dad, William Vincent Clark, remained stoic right to the end, and he never burdened his young son with what was about to happen. My father was a fighter and remained so. In large part, he took this battle on all on his own, and that is how he died, all alone. Now, I have seen God's hand at work, so when I write that my dad died alone, I know that he didn't, and that brings great comfort to me. But my dad did die without the presence of his earthbound family, and I can't change that. However, what I have described wasn't the life altering and changing event that I outlined at the beginning.

Prior to my dad being found dead in his apartment, he called me. I still remember the conversation as though it were no more than five minutes ago. Perhaps appropriately and in the vein of God's infinite wisdom, on a dreary and rainy afternoon, I answered the phone to listen to my dad for the last time on this earth. I didn't say much as my father seemed to try to convince me that everything in life would be okay, and that I was tough enough to handle adversities, no matter what they were. Above all, my dad with a weakening voice exclaimed, "Keep your faith in the Lord!" "He guides!" Finally, and this is what I regret more than anything I have done, or didn't do, my dad told me that he "loved me," and on the other end of the phone, where I was, there was silence. At the time when my dad needed me most, I wasn't there. At a time when my dad needed to hear that I loved him too, I failed to speak. We hung up, and I continued about my daily business. Several days later, my mom and Aunt Eileen, a sweetheart of an aunt, came in the front door with the life-changing news. It was then that I put all of the pieces of the puzzle together. All that lecturing, my dad's stumbling into the table when I went to get the check at his apartment, he knew that he was dying! I distinctly remember staring out our front window that day and asking myself how I could have missed all of that? How could I have failed to connect the dots? It took me a few years to discover that I wasn't supposed to. Not at that moment anyway. God had a plan, and his timing was perfect!

Prior to my dad's death, and as I mentioned earlier, my parents had split up. My mom suffered from several internal conflicts and mental issues, and life in the house was oftentimes very difficult. I became depressed and terribly introverted-- I mean to the extent that I did not want to be seen in public. Whenever I was outside playing and would hear a car or people approaching, I would either hide behind the bushes in our front yard, or I would run back into the house. I quit all activities and had almost no friends. As you can imagine, the future did not seem bright to me. Remember now, this was all before my father had died. In fact, it was my dad's death that changed everything around.

The night of being informed of the news, I sat outside on my front steps feeling the guilt and shame of not doing and saying what I should have. I began to realize that what I regretted the most was not what I had done, but what I didn't do, and I believe that is true for most of us. We all do things that we wish we could take back, but those are usually forgivable…and changeable. What we don't do though must be corrected with a different and usually more difficult process, and that's assuming that the failure to act can be overcome, because sometimes it can't. In my case, I could do something about it, but the thought of it scared me to no end. I knew that what I was feeling wasn't good, and I had the awareness of self to realize that I had to make amends. I also knew that I had to do something that would both show my dad, who no doubt was looking down, that I did in fact love him while simultaneously serving as a method of redemption for me. Given the courage that my dad had demonstrated during this time, I felt that whatever it was that I did, had to show strength too. It was on those cold concrete front porch steps that I realized I would do the very thing that I was most afraid of. The kid that was so self-conscious that he avoided contact with people at all cost would publicly speak by delivering the eulogy. I went inside and told my mother of my intended brazen move. Her response was one of protection. She had seen what was going on and must have thought to herself that I was nuts. My mother reminded me that the church would be filled, and to a large extent, with the neighborhood people that I wanted the least to do with. I already knew that, and I told her so. It took some time, but she finally agreed. I took things a step further by deciding to add my own words to the reading, a fact that I withheld from everyone until it was too late for them to intervene. The truth is that I think everyone was so nervous for me that they failed to notice that I had authored my own material, and that was fine with me. I wasn't looking for attention or praise. I wanted, in my own mind, to set the record straight. This was a moment between my God, my dad, and myself. During the funeral, I remember sitting, praying, and waiting for the nod to approach the alter. I stared up at the crucifix and asked for the strength to overcome the weaknesses that I showed just days before, and the Lord delivered. I didn't hesitate, stutter, or miss a beat. As I stepped down from my short presentation, I realized that a new me had just been born. What I didn't realize at the time was that the new me could not have come about without the brutal failure several days prior. Out of our darkest hours can come the sweetest of redemptions, but they won't happen unless you step into the face of your fears. You won't be able to defeat what you refuse to challenge.

Please don't misunderstand me. If I could go back in time and make some adjustments, I would do so faster than the blink of an eye, but that just isn't possible. Over time, I came to realize that I never lost on that day of silence, nor did I fail. The mistakes made served only to catapult me to what I love to do the most and that is motivationally speak and write, and my dad's death also provided a way to become closer to my family. My uncles Art, Gerry, and Bob, and aunts Eileen, Alice, and Hellen, were of great support during those days. God knew where he wanted me, and He made sure that I got there. Unfortunately, sometimes the roads taken are filled with pain, and that has to be all right. During these times though, you need to remind yourself that everything will be okay. Wherever there is pain and turmoil, there is also possibility. It's easy to get lost in the despair of the moment, but regain your composure; clear the fog in your head, and look for the opportunity, because I can assure you that one is either there waiting for you, or is soon to be coming. Stay strong, be faithful, and continue to persevere. Better days are on the way, but sometimes you have to rise above the clouds of hardship to find them.

Affirmations:

1) Today I will tell those important in my life how much they mean to me.
2) Today I will speak. Being embarrassed over saying something kind and positive is better than the regret of silence.
3) Today I will overcome failure by looking for the opportunity hidden within it.

CHAPTER 2

Choosing Your Mindset

Here I am at age 15. This was taken at the Old York Barbell Club in Pennsylvania. I used to take the bus down from Binghamton, NY and train with my coaches Leo Totten and Dick Smith. They taught me a lot more than just how to lift weights!

* I want to preface this essay with the fact that there may be many reasons for anxiety and fear. If you have been battling with this, you might want to see a doctor. You should feel no shame in this whatsoever! Believe me, you are not alone, and you will be all right! As a world champion athlete, I received mental coaching from some of the nation's best psychologists. In the world of athletics, we call it mental coaching, but it's really counseling. Regardless of what society wants to label it, there should be no negative stigmas attached to seeking help. I did it, and I'm glad. Please, take care of yourself and do what is necessary to be at your very best!

Fear and anxiety can be crippling. If not managed, they have the power to snatch defeat out of the sure hands of victory and sabotage the best of efforts and plans. Fortunately, you have more control over them than you may presently think, and my goal here is to illustrate that.

Not only does every athlete face these two enemies, often on a daily basis, but so do most people in every other walk of society as well, and it isn't easy. There's the fear of failure, the fear of injury, the fear of embarrassment, and I can go on and on, but you get what I'm driving at. Making matters worse is the fact that anxiety travels with fear. If one is present, the other will be in the near vicinity. They are always together, and this is the undeniable truth of what people who want to succeed must confront and overcome. But I have great news-- fear and anxiety can be mastered! Before I pass along a few motivational stories, I want you to understand a few things that may be of help.

First, you can only concentrate on one thing at a time, and I'm told that this physiological rule applies to states of emotion as well. In other words, it is impossible to focus on confidence and anxiety at the same time. Along the same lines, my understanding is that a person cannot be happy and sad at the same time either. Secondly, per the staff at the Olympic Training Center, there is absolutely no physiological, or physical, difference between the negative state of mind produced by anxiety and the positive state of mind manufactured by excitement. In both cases, the blood pressure and heart rate rise, there may be dryness of the mouth, and even a "shaky feeling" sometimes referred to as "weakness of the knees" occurs. Third, a great majority of our fears never come true. Someone once said that "fears are false evidences appearing real," and I think that's true in most cases. To that extent, you are wasting your time worrying about things that won't ever come to pass. Think about this for a minute or two. Almost all of our fears relate to the future, and we compound them by allowing our imaginations to run free. It might even be that fears are nothing more than the product of an undisciplined mind, and that is something that we can improve upon. At times, however, anxiety, fear, and depression are not the result of an undisciplined mind. When there is a true disorder, biological factors are at play, and a qualified medical professional needs to be seen. You shouldn't be embarrassed to do so either. In fact, I think there is more shame in knowing that you need some help and being too proud to accept it. It's probably selfish as well, because those in your circle will directly feel the effects of your decisions. On a quick side note, my personal doctor, Sanjiv Patel, an incredible human being, explained the biological side of this to me. I'm paraphrasing here, but Dr. Patel says that "anxiety may be the result of a brain chemistry imbalance." In short, there are issues with neurotransmitters, or brain chemicals, like norepinephrine and serotonin, and medicine can be of great assistance. Regardless of whether or not you suffer from a diagnosed disorder, it's your attitude and mindset that will determine how you respond.

To make this point a little clearer, your body reacts the same way to a fun activity like sex as it does to an unpleasant experience like going to the doctor's office for an exam. Again, your physiological response is the same, but I bet your mental approach isn't. Most of us don't need any help getting excited over sex, but I used to hate going to the doctor's because I was afraid, and I was afraid because of what I focused on! I used to think about what could go wrong, and that is the very breeding ground of anxiety. Anxiety is misdirected thought, and thoughts come from the mind. Anxiety and fear are often the result of choices made. The good news is that we have the power to change what we think about. We have the power to choose our thoughts and concentrate on more positive outcomes. When we dwell on positives, we begin to get excited. Whereas anxiety yields an unpleasant and impending feeling of doom, excitement produces the feeling that something good is about to happen. When we are excited, we are looking forward to the upcoming event, and I think that one of the best ways to do this is to concentrate on the opportunity at hand.

Years ago, I was competing with the USA team in an international event. A full 100% tear to the teres major of my shoulder forced me to take only one bench press. Subsequently, I fell behind as we headed into the deadlift portion of the meet. It came down to my final attempt on the deadlift, and if I made it, I would not only win, but set a new world record as well. If I missed, I would have to settle for second. As I sat in my chair in another room away from the competition platform waiting to be called, I began focusing on how I had the chance to do something that years earlier I could only dream of. Every time my mind began drifting away to unpleasant thoughts of defeat and injury, I refocused and brought it back, and that takes practice. Choosing excitement instead of anxiety may sound easy, but it isn't. You must discipline yourself to do this, and it will take effort, so keep working at it. Remember, we are all a work in progress, and

God is never done with us. I can promise you that those with the strongest minds are only so because of the numerous times that they had failed in the past and learned from it. Failure to succeed is not the enemy, but failure to learn from it is. Make an oath to yourself that you will never quit. Make an oath to yourself that you will learn from your mistakes, try again using better strategies, take control of your emotions, and get excited over the opportunities available to you. That's exactly what winners do.

I remember hearing a very relevant story several years ago, and it helps to illustrate the power of a resolved mind. A kicker for a football team missed one field goal and one extra point during regulation play. The missed point after the last touchdown would have actually been enough to win the contest, but the miss inevitably forced overtime. The two teams battled for several minutes until the team that the kicker in question was on found itself in field goal range. With a fourth down and one-yard-to-go situation, the coach called out to the kicker. Since the kicker had already missed two attempts, the coach wanted to ask him how he felt. What's interesting is that when the coach called for him, he wasn't there. The kicker was already on the field warming up for the attempt. When the coach witnessed his level of confidence, he allowed him to try. The kick sailed through the uprights for a victory. Afterwards, the athlete was asked how he handled the earlier disappointments. The kicker said that he realized what he could do better, and from that point on, he focused on success and not failure. Although he may have used different wording, that focus on success is also a focus on excitement! Just like anxiety, fear and failure are found together, so are excitement, strength, and success.

When it comes right down to it, anxiety and excitement are often times a matter of choice, but you can only pick one at a time. You can't control everything that happens, but you can control how you respond, and you can certainly control what emotions you choose to empower and reinforce. It takes practice, so don't be discouraged if you find yourself falling into negativity and anxiety from time to time, but refocus as soon as possible. Anxiety only exists in the mind and almost always involves fear of the future. They are very likely, however, to be illusions and not real, so don't give in to them. Maybe you need some help from the medical field, and maybe you don't. Do what you need to in order to take control of your mind and get excited, because doing so is a gateway to better days and future success.

Affirmations:

1) Today I will look for the good in every situation.
2) Today I will choose to look into the future with hope and excitement for the incredible possibilities that it presents.
3) Today I will take control of those things that I can and make it the best day possible.
4) Today I will reject the illusions of fear and anxiety and proceed on the best path possible.
   - Some fears are very legitimate. Those are not the type that I refer to as "illusions." Your doctor and common sense should be of value with those determinations

CHAPTER 3

Fractions

This picture was taken at a meet in Maryland where I set
the world record deadlift with no belt or super suit.

At one time or another, we all feel as though we are miles away from our
goals and dreams. I'm going to give you some hope today because you
might just be a lot closer than you think. One of the most valuable tools
for an athlete or coach is video analysis. My Olympic Weightlifting coach
Leo Totten, used to break down my technique in this manner, and it served
me incredibly well. Back in the day, we would record ourselves training by
using a VHS tape and then play it back on the VCR/TV. Leo would tape a
piece of tracing paper over the television and map the trajectory of the bar
as I lifted. This was highly useful because we could compare the pathway

and movement of my bar to that of other, more experienced, and better lifters. However, it wasn't until many years later that the great magnitude of this tool was truly realized.

I was preparing, with total commitment, for the World Championships and was looking to set several drug free world records in the 90 KG weight class. Included among my world record aspirations was a lofty deadlift that would exceed the 700 pound barrier. Although I was routinely handling 650 pounds, 710 kept getting stuck at the height of about two inches above my knees, and in powerlifting, that means failure. Several lifters at the gym told me that 710 was just too heavy and that it was a strength issue, but I didn't think so. I honestly felt as though I was strong enough, and I kept telling myself that. But, I did not dismiss the obvious difference between 650 and 710 pounds, and it seemed as though I was another year and a half away from reaching my benchmark. It was very frustrating, and I was becoming more desperate! The World Championships were drawing closer, and time was getting shorter, so I decided to film myself training. I was hoping that I would find some glaring and easily fixable error that would provide the cure for the 710 pound deadlift disease. As a teacher, I have access to a number of sources and experts, so I went to a colleague that also doubles as a professional photographer. He set me up with the equipment needed to record, and with the additional help of several of my students, I headed into the school's weightroom for action. Once again, 710 was a no-go, but I did get the recording that I needed to analyze my technique.

That night, I loaded the VHS tape into the VCR and began tracing the trajectory, or movement, of the bar. I didn't find any glaring errors in my technical execution, but I did find what would equate to a microscopic flaw in the timing of my lift. Sometimes, even a small error can have a large impact, and the inverse can also be true. What I noticed was that, with heavier weights, I failed to push my hips forward at the exact moment that the bar cleared my knees! I failed to do this with 650 pounds, too, but I was able to overcome the technical deficiency with brute strength. However, to break the 700 pound barrier, I needed everything to be working at full capacity, and that included not only strength, but intelligence, and technical execution too. Now, when I mention that I wasn't pushing my hips through at the exact moment the bar cleared my knees, I am referring to a distance of about 1/2 of an inch. That's how close I was to being technically perfect, a mere 1/2 of an inch. But it was that tiny 1/2 inch that made a sixty pound difference. The subsequent correction led to a new world record, and one that I was quite proud of. This is what I meant earlier when I stated that, "Sometimes we believe that we are miles away from where we want to be, but we are really much closer than we think!"

A friend of mine is an exceptional golfer, and we were both invited to play at a charity event. Prior to this, I had never golfed, and it showed! With each subsequent shot of inadequacy, I laughed and told my partner, "Look how far away I am!" He laughed too, but when he got done, he did some explaining. "Joe" went on to say that it looks like the ball is a "mile away," but looks can be deceiving. He explained further by stating that if I adjust my swing and strike the ball with a different part of the club, I'll end up much closer. Now, the striking part of the club is only a few inches long, and I was making contact about an eighth of an inch away from where I should have been. That's all it took, an eighth of an inch adjustment. I still wasn't going to make the pro tour, but I did greatly improve. I could add many other stories to this one as well. Some of these anecdotes relate to job interviews, and others are about scores on tests, but in the end, they all share the same lesson. Sometimes, it isn't enough to just try harder. You have to try harder the right way. It's a matter of strategy, not just effort. Prior to this, I never realized just how similar powerlifting, golf, and life in general really are. No matter what you are trying to accomplish, you may actually be closer than you think, so before you quit or give up, take a good look at yourself and see if there are any small corrections that can make big differences. Your dream goals might be no more than a fraction of an inch away!

Affirmations:

1) Today I will choose to problem solve and overcome.
2) Today I will step back and look at reality. I will either recognize that I am much closer than I originally thought to victory, or that I need to re-strategize. Either way, I will pursue excellence!
3) Today I will recognize that trying harder might not be enough to attain success. Today I will optimize my efforts by giving 100% in the most efficient and strategic ways.

CHAPTER 4

Bullseye

Here is a photo from *Strength and Power USA*. It may take years and years, but hard work eventually pays off.

I'm not sure exactly how the following was stated or where I was when I heard it, but it sure made sense to me. Even though the wording has been altered, the idea expressed in the next few sentences isn't mine, and it breaks the honor system to present it as otherwise. In any event, too many people hit exactly what they aim for, but their standards are set so low that the result equates to mediocrity, or even worse, poor performance. Very little comes from shooting for average and nailing it! Think about it. What successful coach, teacher, or boss really appreciates average? Conversely, champions in all walks of life, be it in athletics, business, healthcare, or whatever, set challenging goals and work towards them. Winners understand the frustrations and difficulties that lie ahead but willingly accept them because they know that greatness will not result from weak effort or low standards.

Vince Lombardi was quoted as saying, "Perfection is not attainable, but if we chase perfection we can catch excellence!" The truth is that no one would care what Vince Lombardi had said if he hadn't demanded such extremes of himself and reached the levels of victory that he did. Success commands respect, and everyone wants to attain it, but I'm not convinced that many people are willing to pay the necessary and market price for it. In this context, the phrase "market price" refers to the levels of dedication, commitment, and sacrifice that will be needed to reach the desired goals.

During my motivational speeches, I like to talk about why I think hunger is an essential prerequisite for success. It is hard to have a desire for something extra when you already have everything you need and want! Sometimes that hunger is derived from absent or missing needs, such as love, and other times it comes from a lack of material goods. Regardless of how it materializes, motivation is the cornerstone of achievement.

When I was 14 years old, many things that most people would consider necessities were missing from my life. My dad had died, we were monetarily poor, and I fought with both anxiety and depression, so I was desperate for any success that I could get ahold of. I thank the Lord, because I was about to find it! I was lifting weights to make my football game better, and I thought that an Olympic Weightlifter named Joe Gazdik who was training at the same gym, might be able to assist me. It was Mr. Gazdik that introduced me to one of the sports that I love, and I will always be thankful to him for that! Despite my having just started training with Joe,

I decided that, on New Year's Eve in 1983, weighing about 170, I was going to power clean 275 pounds. I had little idea, technically, of what I was doing, but at this stage of my athletic development, the desire for success far outreached any level of common sense that I may have had. I was told early on by Joe to keep a very detailed and accurate training journal, and I fanatically did so. I'm glad that I did. Whenever I feel as though I need a little psychological lift, I refer back to that special day and my state of mind becomes elevated.

I attempted and failed with the 275 pounds a total of five times at the gym, and I would have kept going if it weren't for Joe commanding that I stop. Joe told me that he was pleased with the fact that I wouldn't quit, but he schooled me as to why the risks of continuing to fight with this weight overmatched the benefits. What Joe didn't know was that I had weights in my basement, too, and that I planned on resuming my personal war the minute I got there. And it wasn't hard, because my basement walls were adorned with motivational thoughts and photos, and one of the most treasured was an essay written by one of my powerlifting coaches, multiple world champion, and fellow Hall of Famer, Larry Bucchioni, entitled "Persisting." In short, the piece is about never quitting and how the "rewards of competition (as well as in life) come at the end, not at the beginning!" Properly focused, I loaded the bar to the same 275 pounds and started again.

I failed over and over, this time, up to the count of seven. At that point, I decided that a little more strategy was needed. Given my lack of training knowledge and understanding at that time and age, I thought that ten minute rests between attempts was reasonable. So, I set my mother's kitchen timer and started the procession of insanity. According to my December 31, 1983 journal entry, the grudge match lasted for nearly four hours! The page that it is written on is stained with the blood from my then 14 year old hands. Despite the fact that my palms had swelled and split open, I finally succeeded on the 30th attempt, and it was worth every bit of the pain, suffering, and frustration. The 275 pounds, by the way, was almost inconsequential. Although and at the time it was a personal best by 20 pounds, it was the effort that mattered the most. I had tested myself beyond what was normal. At that point, and this is the truth, I knew that I had the necessary drive and toughness to be successful in weightlifting, as well as in life, but I would not have made that discovery without setting the high standard that I did. Without that pursuit of relative excellence, December 31, 1983 would have been just another New Year's Eve. In all honesty, the feeling of accomplishment that day closely rivaled that of winning a world championship. On a side note, I question whether or not most people are willing to pay that kind of price. In my case, I was desperately searching for something positive, and I had found it, but I don't know if I would have pursued it to that extent if all of my needs were being fulfilled. The fact is that they weren't being met, and it was out of that necessity that came the hunger for something better. This is why, during my talks, I caution people not to prematurely try to escape their problems. The operative word is "prematurely." Often times, there are great opportunities hidden in our struggles, and they frequently serve as blessings, not curses. However, if you aren't actively looking, you won't find them! Don't pray to get relief from your problems, pray for the strength to effectively deal with them! This is the essence of mental toughness, and if you can master it, everything becomes a point of advantage. By the way, I decided to share my story because I wanted to illustrate the point that "normal" people can climb out of their personal valleys of difficulty just as well as celebrities. It's important to remember that, despite their fame and status, superstars are people too, oftentimes dealing with the very same issues that the rest of us fight with.

Because of legalities, I am unable to mention the name of the man whose story this belongs to, but it certainly illustrates what I have been trying to get across. One famous actor was so financially strapped that he could no longer pay his rent. Intensifying the situation was the fact that he had a child on the way. But again, out of this adversity came opportunity. Desperate for income, he sat down and wrote the script for a particular movie in an amazing four days, but what is even more incredible was the very gutsy measure that he imposed on Hollywood production companies. He could have compromised his standards and taken the highest proposals that came, and there were several, but he didn't. In fact and because he was so convinced that he had a bright future as an actor, he turned down the most lucrative offers presented. "Rob" insisted that he get to play the lead role in the film, and many companies rejected that caveat! He stuck to his guns, though, and that was an act of faith. It served him well! Turns out, he became one of the biggest action stars ever, but it might not have come to pass if he had set his standards lower, hit the bullseye, and allowed someone else to play the lead part! Becoming a champion doesn't just pop out of nothing. It takes more often than not, years of 100% commitment, and it all starts with goal setting because without a predestined path and point of arrival, we're bound to get lost. Regardless of the level of measure that we aspire to, if we can see it in the mind, it's possible to get it in the hand. At what and how high are you aiming?

Affirmations:

1) Today I will face my fears associated with failure and pursue personal excellence.
2) Today I will not only see myself as a champion, but I will actively engage in what is needed to become one.
3) Today I will recognize that low standards yield an unproductive and false victory. Today I will recognize and pay the price of setting my standards high, because doing so provides the opportunity to earn self-respect.

CHAPTER 5

Seeing Through the Eyes of Faith

BILL CLARK
State, National, and World Champion
State, National, and World Record Holder

One of my only regrets is never taking a camera to competitions. I worried that taking pictures might distract me from my mission. As such, the only pictures that I have from events are those that others took. The photographers were either kind enough to send them to me or I found them in magazines. Not taking your own pictures though, can leave you looking like this!!

Two days before boarding an airplane to fly to the United States National Championships in North Carolina I came down with strep throat. I immediately called my coach and made him aware of the situation. In addition to telling me to drink plenty of fluids and rest, he also reminded me of my past and that I had been through plenty of worse things before (and overcame them). Before ending the call, he reminded me to "see through the eyes of faith." As it applies here, faith is the ability to see something in the eye of the mind before it actually occurs, and both positive and negative thinking take faith. Although they share some commonalities, these two mindsets take two very different paths.

Negative thinking is the belief, or faith, that an event is doomed to failure, while positive thinking is the faith that things will turn out well. My coach new all too well that the mind is an incredibly powerful tool and could be used to overcome exceptionally difficult situations and odds. Back in my Olympic Weightlifting days and while staying at either the Regional Training Center in York, PA or one of the Olympic Training Centers, I was taught mental imagery and mind control techniques, and they work. In fact, I believe that my mental approach to the National Championships that year played a paramount role in my winning. Coach Rob routinely had his blood pressure taking equipment handy and monitored mine throughout the day's events. Blood pressure, by the way, is not just an indicator of cardiovascular health; it can also be used to check states of mind, as well. When an individual is mentally and emotionally calm and relaxed, the blood pressure is lower, and that conserves energy. Conserved energy can then be released when needed. During moments of down time in the competition, I would imagine myself on a beach in Hawaii. I could actually hear the water and feel the warmth of the sun. In my mind, I was there. My blood pressure, during the second biggest Powerlifting meet of the year, was no higher than it was the night before in the hotel. Right before heading onto the platform to engage in an attempt, I would shift my thinking to the type that would be needed for a search-and-destroy mission, and I would then visualize a successful world record lift. The moment I stepped away from the competitive stage, I went back to my imagined get-away on the beach. This allowed me, at conscious will, to control my energy and thinking, thus helping me to maintain an optimal overall state. That day, while suffering from strep throat, I set two national records and one world record en-route to winning the 198 pound weight class.

To be at their best, champions of all kinds, be it in athletics, healthcare, or business, must train the mind. I think this is a good rule of thumb to assume; the mental state can overcome the physical state, but the physical state won't override the mental. In other words and as Henry Ford once said, "If you think you can or you think you can't, you're right!" It's the mind and its visions that drive the bus of destiny. I believe that people are inherently negative, and as such, it will take lots of work to be able to consistently visualize positive outcomes, and that is the very essence of seeing through the eyes of faith. The good news is that anyone can become better at activating productive, as opposed to counter-productive, faith. This is the main goal behind the mental training that athletes engage in. But, it isn't just for people in training, it's for everyone. I used the same exact mental training program from when I was at the Olympic Training Center in order to prepare for a job interview. Mental toughness is very versatile. For those that have had stress-filled lives, you will have to re-route your thinking and begin to orient your brain and associated central nervous system toward better thoughts. Now, if you're thinking, because of your difficult past, that it's too late to start thinking the right way, you're wrong! In fact, I think it's too late not to start. The past belongs in the rear view mirror of your life's car. Begin looking out the front windshield, and start investing in your future, because things can, and with the right approaches, will, get better.

You may have already read that when I was a kid, around the age of 12, my life was in disarray. At that stage, I hadn't been trained to see through the eyes of faith, and therefore I greatly worried about what would become of me. My dad had just died, and my mother battled with a number of mental issues, some of which required hospitalization. Because of these circumstances, and much of the time, I was either alone, or fended for myself. I would sometimes buy my own groceries, make my own dinners, and do my own laundry, etc. Things progressed to the extent that the Department of Social Services intervened. I was told that my situation probably dictated that I be removed from my house and placed into foster home care. The social worker assigned to my case was a man named Brian. He was a kind guy, and I always felt as though he was genuinely trying to help me. When he made the suggestion that I be moved, I flat out told him that I would leave wherever they put me, and I would come back home. No one would be able to stop me. That was pretty brash talk for a 12 year old, especially for back in those days, but Brian listened, and

I will always be thankful to him. Despite what my mother was fighting against, I always and instinctively knew that she had the best of intentions and was still motivated by love and that was what kept me there. Staying home, however, did not relieve the situation, and I still worried almost constantly about what the future held for me. I recognized, even back then, that I was well behind the curve of what would be considered normal. The other kids had new clothes, their families were together, and they seemed to have all of the advantages that I wished for. Sometimes, comparison to others can rob you of your happiness, and it's often best to avoid doing this. When you're 12, however, this philosophy doesn't usually come to mind. More importantly, and when I look at how far I have come, I realize that I shouldn't have worried so much. It was wasted energy, and I wish that I had had more faith back then.

That is the message that I would like to send to you. Maybe you've got some things challenging you today. Be faithful; you will be okay! You may not be able to immediately change your circumstances, but you can certainly change the way that you view them. Seeing through the eyes of faith means that you can look into the future and see yourself as not only successful, but far beyond where your present circumstances have you. See yourself in a different environment, surrounded by people who care, and at the top of your game. To get out of your present situation though, you are going to have to find your gifts and talents, and you probably won't find them on the Playstation or cell phone. You have to engage in life, and search. Have fun doing it too, because no one can do a better job of taking care of you than you. As I said earlier, I worried a lot. I wish I knew then what I know now. Seeing through the eyes of faith allows you to do just that. Change what's in your mind, and you can begin to change your circumstances. It won't happen though, until you start building upon your visions, so get going. I don't know what your path is, but I do know that you have one. Start working toward a better life today. Remember, it's not where you start that matters, it's where you finish!

Affirmations:

1) Today I will recognize that attaining success is a process and that it may take years to do so. I will acknowledge my small steps of

success because it is those minor but very significant details that add up to the bigger victories that we set out to achieve.

2) Today I will see myself beyond the present circumstances and situations that I am currently in. I will see myself as a victor.

3) Today I will begin to change the patterns of my thinking and start to create the person that I know I have the potential to become.

CHAPTER 6

Following Your Dreams...

The process of becoming better than you were the day
before doesn't end when practice does.

I was in the 7th grade when I decided that I was going to become a
Division 1 football player. Having watched numerous professional and
college football games with my dad, cousins, and friends, I knew it was
something that I wanted to pursue. I grew up in Syracuse, NY where
football was and is a very popular sport to play. We would play football
anywhere and often. However, it would be awhile before I could participate
in organized football because I did not meet the weight requirement to
play Pop Warner at the time. So, I was left on my own to hone my skills.

I would play countless games throughout my neighborhood and the city. I was one of those kids who always carried a football with him, looking for a game to start or get involved in. I would play every position in hopes of getting better so that when my opportunity came to play organized football I would be ready to go! It wasn't until I was in the 8th grade that I was able to get my first taste of organized football on the freshman team. After two years of freshman football, I got called up as a sophomore to play on the varsity team. Very excited about the opportunity to participate in the game that I was falling more and more in love with, I began to work even harder to reach the very ambitious goal I'd set back in the 7th grade of earning a Division 1 football scholarship.

Syracuse and the surrounding area at who time had several athletes that were getting opportunities to go to college on scholarship and play their sport. I knew I wanted to be added to that list. I was very fortunate in that when I entered high school, I was able to connect with other guys who shared my same dream of playing major college football. As we got older, we began to realize the financial burden that could be lifted off of our parents if we were able to receive scholarships to go to college, and that motivated us even more! We made a commitment to each other to work hard enough to get a scholarship offer. That decision would set us on a course that forced us to work hard every day! And it put in place a level of accountability that kept us all focused and dedicated. It put in place a partnership of several individuals who all thought alike and wanted to work toward the same end goal of getting a scholarship. We would spend countless hours in the weight room and on the track and running hills. We would go to various camps to learn more and compete and then come back and share what we learned from our experiences. We all wanted to "get some ink" and I'm not talking about tattoos. We referred to "get some ink" as seeing our name in the sports section of the newspaper. That was the "BIG" thing at the time, making it in the sports section of the newspaper! And, we all knew that in order for that to happen, we would have to outwork the competition. I'll be the first admit, that whole "outwork the competition" phrase raised the level of competition to new heights! We all did multiple sports because it was encouraged, and it kept us together. I participated in football and track and field. Other guys participated in basketball, lacrosse and track and field as well. Because the level of competition was so high, we had opportunity! Remember, at the end of the day, that's all anyone can ever ask for is an opportunity!

As I mentioned earlier, guys were going all over the country to play football, but some decided to stay home and play at Syracuse University. Others would go on to play for Army, Navy, Boston College, Boston University, Wagner, Tennessee, Michigan, Ohio State, CW Post, Cornell, Hofstra, LSU, Penn State, Notre Dame, and the University of Buffalo. One skipped college altogether and went into the NFL. I would have an opportunity to go pretty much anywhere in the country on a football or track scholarship. I chose to play football at the University of Alabama. This was a true blessing for me in that the University of Alabama was my #1 choice. And, despite all of the naysayers and believe me, there were a bunch who told me I would never play at Alabama or who told me I was too short to play at the Division 1 level, I proved them all wrong! Why?? Because this was about me chasing my dreams and not listening to people who had given up on theirs! I surrounded myself with the right types of people, people who would encourage me when needed or hold me accountable. And I did the same for them. It was about me making the sacrifice to do the work needed to get me to that level and keeping my eye on the prize!

Once at the University, one of my goals was to contribute to the glorious history of Alabama football. I finished my career at Alabama as a four-year letterman, three-year starter. I was voted "Lifter of the year," which is an honor bestowed to the team's strongest player. I played in four bowl games, won a Southern Eastern Conference Championship, and was an S.E.C. player of the week vs. L.S.U., an honor I shared with my other offensive linemates. So, my experience at the University of Alabama was exactly how I'd dreamt it would to be, full of hard work, dedication and plenty of blood, sweat and tears. Because I believed in myself and was willing to make sacrifices to follow my dreams, I was able to make them come true!

My advice to you is to never give up! Misery loves company, and those who fail seem to pride themselves on pulling others down with them. Don't let that be you! Start chasing your dreams today. If I can do it, you can too!

Affirmations:

1) I understand that success doesn't come easy, but today I will begin paying the price.
2) Today I will set myself apart from the naysayers and use their negativity as fuel for my journey.
3) Today I will put the love for my chosen craft near the front of my mind and allow this to inspire my actions.

Here I am playing for the University of Alabama. My dream came true!

Another high school picture. Track and field was another love of mine.

PART TWO

Paving Your Path to Victory

Trent and I believe that success is never an accident; it must involve an orchestrated, step-by-step plan. It might even take years to accomplish your goals, but keep celebrating the small steps of progress along the way. The bigger your dreams, the more likely that it will take longer to achieve them, and that is all right because God's timing is always perfect! The champion's life is built upon the details of the plan, and this section includes a number of essays designed to help you do just that. Additionally, we want to help you stay motivated because those that do are much more likely to reap the rewards of their efforts. A famous weightlifter years ago was asked if anyone could break the 500 pound barrier in the clean and jerk. His reply was that it was only impossible until someone did it, and he did! That's a philosophy that we want you to embody.

You are capable of incredible things. The trick is to enjoy what you have a natural aptitude, or talent, for. To realize this you have to search long and hard to find your natural gifts and talents, formulate strategies, and then maximize your efforts. The great news is that you are probably good, maybe even great, at a number of things, so don't feel trapped. About three years ago, I noticed that my son had a natural ability to jump. Jumping is often a very accurate predictor of an athlete's potential for explosive power. Seeing his inherent gift, I asked if he would like me to teach him the techniques of weightlifting and powerlifting. He struggled with this decision until I finally asked him a key question, and it's one that I suggest you also ask yourself. If you knew you could be the best in the world at something that you hated doing, would you still want to do it? My son's answer was, "No," and in it he demonstrated wisdom well beyond his age. Life is way too short to spend doing something unenjoyable. Just as importantly, it is doubtful that anyone could become the best in the world doing something that he or she hates. The level of competition is just too high, and others who have a genuine passion for their craft will be able to outwork those that don't. Of course, the best formula then is to love your work.

Take the time to investigate your areas of potential, and then apply them to the things that you have a true liking for. It's essentially a blending of two separate, but very related traits, and even if others doubt you, have faith in your abilities. No one knows you better than you! I can promise that if I were to have told my peers at Brookside Elementary School when I was ten years old that I would eventually become a world record holder and champion, almost all of them would have laughed at me, and it would have been the same with Trent as well. We are no more special or unique than you. If there is a difference between us however, it is only that we found what we had talent for and then developed it through painstaking efforts. Additionally, we never gave up or quit. Please notice though that any differences come in the form of decisions made and not in talents possessed. You have your own gifts that are awaiting your pursuit, but they will never come to fruition by waiting for them to reveal themselves. You have to start knocking on your own internal doors, and you do that by finding what you love to do. Test yourself to ensure that your talents match. Once you find that connection between love and natural ability, start developing your skill sets. You are born with talent, but skills have to be perfected, and that can only be done through strategic, consistent, committed, and sacrificial practice. Your life from this day forward can be like a story (and one that you write all on your own), but I would like you to try something that I discuss at my seminars. Start your story with the ending first, make it a victorious one, and then put together a plan that leads you there. Visualize where you want to end up, and don't lose sight of that picture, especially when times get tough. We believe that those that can see themselves as winners are more likely to be so. Success comes in all shapes, colors, and sizes. Become the best teacher, doctor, nurse, or whatever, that you can be, and start the process now. Make a pledge to yourself that you are on a new path forever more---a path of longevity, love, happiness, courage, and faith. We hope and pray that our stories and lessons learned help to propel you to the tops of mountains that you never dreamed possible. It is yours for the taking; now go get it!

Affirmations:

1) Today I will begin making the decisions paramount to my becoming the very best.
2) Today I will start searching for those things in life that I love to do, because it is there that my success awaits.
3) Today I will recognize that deciding to be the best and committing oneself to that cause are two very different things. Today I will not only decide to be my best; I will also make the commitment to get it done.

CHAPTER 7

Your Default Setting

Before my series of shoulder injuries, I was blessed to set several national and world records in the bench press. Having great coaching makes a tremendous difference, and I wouldn't have approached this level without them.

Back in the early 2000s, I was at the US National Championships where I had just won my division. National and international powerlifting meets are big events so they are set up over the course of two days. Much the same as wrestling or boxing, weight classes determine who competes against whom and being that I was in the 198 and ¾ pound, or 90 Kg, weight class, I lifted early on Sunday afternoon. I wasn't scheduled to fly back home until Monday morning, so I stayed around to watch some of the heavier lifters. One particular competitor caught my attention. I was standing over by the head official's table making small talk with one of the judges when this lifter handed in his final attempt. In powerlifting, each lifter gets three attempts on the platform for each competitive event (squat, bench press, and deadlift), and he or she must inform the head official as to what weight will be attempted. You can move up in the weight attempted, but you can never go down, so strategy must always be considered. This lifter was never really contending for the championship, but nonetheless, he qualified and routinely arrived in good competitive form. What caught my attention, however, was his *attitude* about the weight being lifted, not the weight itself.

He handed in his third attempt and then told the head official, "I don't know why I'm trying this, I'm never going to make it." He then looked at me and asked, "What do you think, big Bill? Do I have a shot?" I'm sure I don't have to tell you how the attempt turned out. When I bring this example up during my presentations, people seem shocked by how an athlete at that level could think so pessimistically, but the truth is that we all have our moments of doubt. I can assure you that everyone thinks negatively from time to time, even the best of the best. The negative thoughts themselves though are not the problem. The real issue lies in the length of time that we spend meditating on those thoughts. It's the dwelling on the thought that is the issue, not the thought itself. Over time and through the creation of neural-pathways, these thoughts become patterned, and it becomes easier to think this way. It's kind of like making a path to sleigh downhill in fresh snow. The first run is hard, but the second one is easier, and so is the third. After a number of times downhill, the path becomes slicker and slicker and therefore easier to travel on. Your mind operates much the same way, and if you're not careful, you won't even be aware of your own obvious negativity.

Such was the case with this lifter. He immediately approached me after the last failed attempt, and asked if he was even close to making it. I then asked him if he was aware of what he said to the official. Not surprisingly, he said that he wasn't. He was flying on auto pilot, but his auto pilot was negative in nature, and that is exactly what the default setting is all about. It is an auto pilot. When stress and difficulties strike their hardest, we often aren't even aware of what we are doing or what we are saying, and that makes our response all the more important. We want our default settings to be solution oriented and productive. We want our default settings to be positive, and fortunately, with some strategically applied hard work, I think that this is very achievable.

I truly believe that we should never be more concerned with how we appear on the outside than what we believe and have on the inside. Inside us lies the values and ethics that shape our missions and dreams. Those that prioritize appearances over internal processing and outcomes are often forced to react to many situations that come their way because they're not focused on the right things. However, those that follow set principles and guidelines are able to respond and they are always setting themselves up for something better down the road. That is exactly what I want to teach here. Remember, reaction is an untrained and often inappropriate way of dealing with immediate stressors. At best, reactions are ineffective maneuvers, but responses are a trained and ingrained management system. By default and because responses involve proactive thought and strategy, they are superior to reactions in every way. When you hear sports announcers discussing athletic reactions, they are usually wrong. Athletes usually train themselves to do what it is they do and that makes their movement much more responsive than reflexive. That is, they are usually responding not reacting.

I believe that your default setting is a matter of conditioning. I had the best coaches in the world, and they, for lack of a better word, "brainwashed" me to always believe that I could succeed. It really wasn't brainwashing, because for that to occur, one must be unaware that it is happening, and I clearly was. Nonetheless, we spent hours upon hours training the mind, and I am going to share this expertise with you. I have a series of steps to help you change your default setting from negative to positive.

To begin, you need to increase your level of self awareness. Reflect on the example that I used to start this chapter with. The lifter's patterns of thought were so ingrained that he failed to recall his statements of pessimism. You probably won't be able to fix your problem unless you first become aware that one exists. Once you become aware that you are thinking negatively, I suggest that you simply re-direct the voice in your head to something positive. We are not talking now about your emotions. Emotions lie, so do not put your faith in them. I believe that your feelings will eventually catch up with your internal voice anyway, but for starters, I simply want you to start talking to yourself the right way. When you begin to doubt that you have what it takes to get something done, recognize it, and change the voice to say something like, "I can do this. I have been in difficult situations before and came through. I did it before and I can do it again."

This will go a long way to making the necessary change, but there is one more absolutely critical step that you must take. Honestly, I am quite proud to share this next step with you because I have never heard this presented before by anyone else. It is now ours together, and I pray and hope that this helps you as much as it has me. Before getting to this though, I want you to get cleared by your doctor for physical exercise, and then always stay within the parameters that your provider has given. Having said this, I want you to engineer difficult tasks and challenges into your workout schedule. If you don't have a workout schedule, see your doctor and then make one. These challenges will be relative to your levels of conditioning and strength. For a runner that does five miles every other day, he may want to incorporate some difficult hills into the course. If you are healing from a knee injury, you may want to structure challenges into your recovery routine. Again, talk to your health care provider. Regardless of where you are presently at, I want you to write down some sort of a mantra before your challenge. Become familiar with it to the extent that it is memorized. Make it short and meaningful. Throughout your entire workout, and especially during the orchestrated challenge part, repeat your phrase over and over.

I incorporate the running of stairs into my training. It is there that I recite my words, and I change them every week. The words change, but the meaning stays the same. One week, my mantra was a very simple: "Yes I can." With every stride I said this, and I said it aloud. I suggest you do the same. Let your ears here the words too. This is called creating a central nervous system response. In short, we are training ourselves to say, "Yes I can," while others will continue to say, "I don't know why I'm trying this; I'm never going to make it."

The reason that the third step is so important is because we want to be able to, at the snap of a finger, become positive during times of difficulty, but to do this, we need to train ourselves during stress. Granted, it is simulated stress, but your subconscious mind cannot tell the difference between reality and fiction, and it is the subconscious that will most likely be the decision maker during a crisis. That's why I think this works for me. You are training the subconscious to behave the way you want it to. Now, this may take some time, but keep working at it, and I think you'll find a shift in your thinking for the better. Start measuring the distance (in seconds) between when you first start thinking negatively and your ability to speak a positive outcome to yourself. Try to close that gap each time, until your first thought eventually becomes positive, until your first thought is "Yes I can!" Pretty soon your default setting will become one of great expectation, and you'll find that more and more people will be trusting you to be a leader on the team.

Affirmations:

1) Today I will choose to speak to myself in such a way as to maximize my efforts and odds of success.
2) Today I will increase my self-awareness and choose not to react, but instead to respond.
3) Today I will begin training my mind to work for me by dwelling on the great opportunities that the situations of life bring.

CHAPTER 8

Excuses

Excuses are the enemy of future success, and although almost everyone will tell you that they are aware that they are counter-productive and have no redeeming value, most are equally as quick to offer them. It is easy to understand the attractiveness of a well timed and relatively believable excuse. They offer protection to our frail egos. Excuses, at their core, are a redirected focus away from our failures on to something else. We all want the spotlight when things go well, but when we fail, we are quick to redirect that spotlight off of us and onto those excuses that serve to help protect us. Don't confuse excuses with reasons, however. They are two very different things.

Years ago, I was competing at the nationals, and an athlete named Dean was there too. Dean lifted in a weight class well below mine, so we never had to compete against each other, but he was a class act guy and a solid competitor. Dean confessed to me that a couple of nights before the meet he had come down with a pretty tough case of the flu. Dean was not the kind to complain, but it was obvious that he wasn't himself. The next day, Dean performed well but not to his best, and he placed third. He was interviewed by someone later that evening and I recall what he told him. I should mention that Dean was probably the favorite that year in the 165 pound weight class, and a third place finish, although good, wasn't what he wanted or what people in the sport expected. Nonetheless, he responded with grace by first giving full credit to those that bettered him and then by saying that he hadn't taken full control of many of the variables in his life leading to the meet. Dean went on to explain that he stayed out a little too late on a couple of occasions and spent some time in some places where he shouldn't have been, and that cost him. "I didn't fail today," Dean exclaimed. "I failed on several occasions a week earlier. It was those failures that caught up with me today." Dean finished by saying that it wouldn't happen again, and to my knowledge, it didn't.

Notice however, that Dean's words never took the focus off of himself. Everything that he offered that night was reflective in nature. Everything offered provided the necessary means to get better. His words were almost a confession, an admittance of guilt. In essence, Dean was saying, "I blew it." "I know what I did wrong, here it is, and I know how to fix it too." Dean offered reasons, not excuses. Reasons may or may not be productive, but they always keep the focus on you. Excuses are never productive and remove the blame. Going back to the beginning of this chapter, we all know excuses are bad, but I am going to explain why they are much more damaging to your future than you may have first thought.

First off, but not necessarily most important, excuses justify your failure, and in making them create or reinforce a negative response. The main problem with this lies in its deception. The excuse makes you feel better, because it takes the fault off of you and places it on another person, thing, entity, or circumstance. This may make you feel better but it won't make you any better. Directing the blame away from you gives you a viable reason to lose every time. In other words, you have no fear of the pain of loss because it will never be your fault. Ironically, you should almost never be afraid to lose. I know this sounds confusing, but let me elaborate and make this concept clearer. Not being afraid to lose because you gave your absolute best is productive. Not being afraid to lose because you have vowed to never quit is productive. Not being afraid to lose because you realize that you will learn from your past mistakes is productive. Not being afraid to lose because it will always be someone else's, or something else's, fault is unproductive! It's actually worse than that, it's counterproductive! This type of attitude doesn't keep you at your present level of performance. More likely, it sets you back and makes you worse.

Secondly, excuses hand your level of control over to another. In Dean's case, the flu was not the problem. The real issue was what he had done to contract the flu several days earlier. It was his fault, and that's a good thing. Think about it, if something else is to blame, how can it possibly be confronted and fixed by you? The answer is it can't. However, if you are to blame, if you are the reason for the problem, then you are also the answer to the problem. Excuses prevent you from correcting. Excuses stop you from strengthening the weaker areas in your game. In their absence, the power belongs to you! Why would you give that up? I can, with almost 100% certainty, tell you that most champions would not.

I know you don't need another reason to stop using excuses, but I will offer a final third. Excuses hurt your credibility. I have a code that I always try to live by, and that is that I never mention anyone else's name when discussing mistakes made. Mentioning another's name in that context seems cowardly, and therefore, I try to avoid such behavior. In a perfect world, every boss and coach would be both honorable and intelligent enough to never make an error in judgement, but we know that is not possible. Therefore, forgive all as you would like to be forgiven, take responsibility for what you can, and choose to make your game better through self-correction. Excuses are the enemy of advancement, so take a pledge from now on to never make them. In the end, I think you will be happy that you did.

Affirmations:

1) Today I will take ownership of everything that I do. I will look not to pass blame to others, but instead look for ways to raise my own level of performance

2) Today I will choose to be productive in my handling of failures and disappointments. It is in this way that our failures will turn to victories.

3) I will live in such a manner today as to ensure success tomorrow.

CHAPTER 9

When Opportunity Knocks

Training the mind by training the body is a great way to be
ready for opportunities when they come. Schedule tough
moments into your day and tell yourself, "Yes I can!"

This is the tale of two very different people headed in very different
directions. In order to keep people protected, I am going to change the
names of those involved. The identities are really irrelevant anyway because
it is their stories that provide us with a framework and model of what to
do and what not to do when "opportunity knocks."

Bob was a talented lifter who competed in the lesser weight classes.
Exactly which one I no longer recall, but he had excellent speed, technique,
strength, and potential. Everyone could see the bright future that lay ahead
of him. Although Bob lived on the West Coast, we became semi-friends
and kept in touch through the mail and telephone. Back in 1986, there
were no cell phones to text with, and email hadn't been invented yet, so

communication could be a bit challenging. Nonetheless, we maintained some connection. Bob and I were both selected to attend an under 23 national squad training camp to be held at The Olympic Training Center in Colorado Springs, Colorado, and it was there that my "spider-sense" began to tingle. Up to this point, we had seen one another at events around the country, but because we were athletes and our focus was on competition, our friendship remained superficial. At the Olympic Training Center, we stayed in the same complex, trained together, ate together, and relaxed together as a team. That type of environment allows people to learn about one another, and subsequently, grow either closer or further apart.

Bob quickly showed that he was a troubled young man who had difficulty following directions, the best of advice, and even orders. I considered it a privilege to be part of any United States Team, and as such, I followed everything that the coaching staff suggested. Not to blow my own horn, but I don't believe there ever existed an athlete more coachable than I, and it totally boggled my mind as to how someone else could act contrary to my system of beliefs. I never once thought that I was in such possession of talent that I could afford to be anything other than the hardest worker possible, and that attitude helped me to win World Championships and set World Records (in Powerlifting). I believe that one of the quickest ways to become Number Two is to always assume you'll be Number one, and I never did. For that matter, I still don't. God directs me on the path of achievement, and knowing that is humbling, but Bob never seemed to figure that out, and it cost him dearly. I remember walking through the complex on our way to lunch after a particularly tough training session, and listening to him say that the coaches couldn't touch him and that they needed him for the next big international meet (which was scheduled to be held in Germany). I was shocked that anyone could have this type of mindset.

Later that evening, I called my coach and legend in the Olympic weightlifting world, Leo Totten. Before my departure to Colorado, we had scheduled a time to make contact. On a quick side note of humor, I called right on time as agreed, but it was Colorado time, not Pennsylvania time where Leo was. I had totally forgotten about the difference in time zones and ended up waking both him and his wonderful wife Patty. There again though is the example that the great leaders demonstrate. Leo handled this with such patience and grace, and he kept it together to the extent that he was still able to provide the best advice possible, and that was to distance myself from Bob. Leo went on to explain that the people that we choose to surround ourselves with often dictate who we become. Although it may have looked to an outsider like Bob and I were on the same page, it was becoming clearer to me that we weren't. Not more than a few days later, Bob not only violated the curfew imposed by the coaching staff, but he also proceeded to throw a rock through the windshield of a car while it was stopped at a traffic light. Bob was soon dismissed from camp and sent home. What a shame too, because it wasn't Bob's talent that failed him, it was his lack of self-control. As a teacher, I see this all too often. People who can't or won't take orders from those who know better than they are putting their selfish and false pride ahead of both their potential and performance, and that's a losing philosophy.

Our character defines us to a much greater extent than our talent does. Talent may help us to earn special places, awards, and opportunities, but it is our character that allows us to keep hold of them. In the absence of this, our rewards vanish quickly, and this can lead to a rather brutal and painful fall from grace. That was Bob's problem! He had the talent to go far, but his lack of character short-circuited him. He was sent home from the Olympic Training Center never to be heard from in the strength world again. Unfortunately, I learned years later that he had been sent to prison after several drug dealing charges and convictions. I genuinely hope and pray that Bob is doing better, but either way, his failures do not have to be in vain. We can always learn from what others go through, and in this way he can still serve a significant purpose. I believe that opportunities come our way, every single day, but we have to be ready for them, and on this occasion, a competitor named Joe was.

When Bob was sent out, Joe was brought in. I had seen Joe before, and I even roomed with him for a short while in York, Pennsylvania. Joe was a straight shooter, a hard worker, and a good follower of coaching and directions. Joe came from a household where rules mattered, and this served him well. As unfortunate and insensitive as this may sound, Bob's failure provided the opportunity for Joe to succeed. Bob's loss was Joe's gain, and that is how life's golden chances often come about. Becoming a member of any elite level team is a privilege, not a civil liberty. Nowhere in the United States Constitution does it state that we have the right to represent the nation in international competition. In fact, the founding fathers never guaranteed us much of anything, but they did promise that we would have the right to pursue our dreams and goals, and that is something that we ought never to take for granted. As I look back on those days, I realize how blessed I was. Even though I haven't seen Joe in a long time, I'd bet money that he was thrilled to get the chance that he did. By the same token, Joe was able to take advantage of the open door because he maintained his state of readiness. It's rare that someone is sent home from places like the Training Center. It's equally as rare that someone else is brought in for the purpose of replacement. Joe had no idea that he would be called, but he continued to train as though he would, and he did! But what would have happened if he had allowed the fact that he was not chosen first to dominate his thinking and propel him into a downward spiral of emotions? I can tell you that he wouldn't have lasted long. He would have been in out-of-strength-shape and forced aside for another. It's an irrelevant proposition however, because he was ready. I know that I speak of seeing through the eyes of faith frequently, but it's important to do so again. One of the biggest reasons that things went well was because Joe looked into the future and realized that where he was heading was being formed and molded by what he was doing during those days when he wasn't there. In other words and in the present tense, what we do today dictates where we end up tomorrow. Joe not only knew that, but he lived it too. So, here are the biggest questions that you alone have to answer: First, how will you respond to disappointment? Second, will you be ready when the door of opportunity knocks for you? Bob's character, or lack thereof failed him, and Joe's acted as a propelling force to better things. I can promise you that opportunity will call your name. Sometimes it's a whisper, and sometimes it comes in the form of a loud "bang." In either case, you have to make the most of it. Make a pledge to yourself today, even when it's the soft voice of possibility trying to get your attention, that you will respond accordingly, with determination, and with strength. Work towards your goals today as though the outcome has already been determined because seeing yourself as a champion just might be the very thing that it takes to make it happen!

Affirmations:

1) Today I will appreciate all of the possibilities that present themselves.
2) Today I will live in a way that allows me to take advantage of unexpected and unplanned opportunities
3) I will live for the future by doing all of the right things today.

CHAPTER 10

The Timing of Your Commitments

This is where I pulled my finger out of the socket. Not long after this training session and despite the pain, I set the all-time record in the one handed deadlift.

Your central nervous system (CNS) is designed to keep you safe and out of harm's way. Generally, and I think we can all agree, that's a good thing. However, there might be several fundamental differences between your CNS and the CNS response that you have created through repetitively reinforcing bad habits. Take smoking for example. At first, your CNS will rebel against the act of smoking by making you feel ill. Your pulse will probably increase, as will your blood pressure, your oxygen blood level will drop, and other symptoms will present themselves too. But keep smoking for ten years and then try to quit. If you are like most people, you will experience a huge number of what will appear to be even worse symptoms (withdrawals) than when you first began your bad habit. In effect, you will have trained your CNS and body to need the terrible, addicting, and death-producing chemicals. However, and always remember this, there is hope. If you trained your CNS to override itself and its included safety measures to now need such things as cigarettes, then you can certainly re-train it to get back in line with good health. Of course, I will always encourage you to see a doctor, but on top of that, I have some advice that may be of help in your fight to get back to being your best. Everybody has something to wrestle with, so we are all in this together. There is no shame in wanting to be better than you were before, and there is no shame in admitting that you have to strategize against some internal enemies in order to get there. There may be shame, however, in recognizing a need to improve and not taking the appropriate action to make it happen. That is something that only you can decide, but I want you to know that I believe in you and your ability to overcome. The human spirit is incredibly powerful and has been a major part of some incredible feats, many of which were never thought possible until they occurred. If you were in front of me right now, you would recognize the sincerity and encouragement in both my tone and inflection when I tell you that you can become more than you ever thought possible.

A couple of years ago, I was preparing to set a world record in the one-handed deadlift. I was training with extreme focus, and I had to because this lift was to take place with a full-sized 7-foot powerlifting bar. Aside from the weight that I would be lifting, balancing the bar until the head referee instructed me to put it down, was more than just challenging. The rules stated that the bar would have to be lifted above the height of the knees and remain steady and balanced until a down signal was to be given, and remember, I was only holding the bar with one hand. About two weeks before the attempt, during a training session, the weight on the bar caused my middle finger to pull out from its socket. I was able to reset it, but the pain was quite severe. Two days before I was to make the lift, my mother went into the hospital and my stress level greatly rose. To make matters worse, I drove to the meet in a sleet storm. All of these things took a tremendous toll on my own CNS. I was fatigued, worried, and in pain, but I still knew that I had what it took to set the record. I write this in all humility, because I will not take credit for much, if any, of my successes in life. I had the best coaches in the world who taught me how to train my CNS and make it work for me instead of against me. I had the support of so many family members, students, and friends, and it never hurts to be directed by almighty God above, and I always have been. The key to making your central nervous system work for you comes in the way that you prep it.

First, you must make a predetermined commitment that you will succeed. To do this, you have to be aware of what you will be getting yourself into. I have seen many people who say that they will make a lift only to drop it at the point of discomfort. To be brutally honest, and I know that this is not intentional, but these people are lying to themselves. They went into the adventure not fully understanding what could happen, and this is often a recipe for failure. Tearing your hand open during a deadlift is very likely, and therefore a lifter ought to be well trained to block out this pain before the attempt occurs. Predetermined commitments involve not getting caught off guard. You know what to expect, you are prepared for it, and therefore, you have a strategy to overcome whatever happens your way, but the key is to prepare and commit prior to the pain and/or discomfort. If you don't make this decision beforehand, your CNS will tell you to quit, and you most likely will, but not because you weren't capable of producing. You will quit because you weren't physically, mentally, emotionally, or spiritually ready. In other words, you weren't prepared.

Getting back to the world record one-handed deadlift, I knew that my finger was going to dislocate again. I was prepared for that to happen even before I stepped on to the competitive platform for the attempt. That's the power of making up your mind before getting started. It did pop out again, but I honestly never felt it. I had conditioned my mind to stay focused on what I needed to do to succeed, not on what could get in my way. Of fundamental importance to success in any endeavor is the fact that you can only and fully concentrate on one thing at a time, but that concentration is a choice. Remember though that your CNS is designed to protect you, and that makes being distracted by any type of pain, be it physical, emotional, mental, or otherwise, a real threat to performance. If you're not careful, pain will pull your attention away from your mission, often causing you to fail. Committing yourself to success prior to the onset of the pain in question helps you to refocus at its first onset. This is of paramount importance because the longer we stay in a divided state of mind, the greater the risk of failure. The inverse is also true. The longer we maintain a unified and single-purposed mind, the more likely it is that we will achieve what we set out to do. Being human, we can expect to fall out of that state of intense concentration, and that is where refocus comes into play. You can do your own math, but the quicker we can refocus back to the goal at hand, the less time we spend in that divided mental state, thus once again increasing the likelihood of a positive outcome. At its core, concentration is a choice, but it must be a trained and practiced choice. Otherwise, you probably won't achieve your goals and reach your true potential. These practiced and trained options, engaged in efficiently and over time, help to create a new CNS response, but this one allows for maximization of effort and could help to propel you to better heights. Having stated this, I never condone self abuse or anything of the like. Please don't hurt yourself. In my case, I knew my finger would eventually heal, but if I were faced with the risk of having life altering injuries, I would never have attempted the lift. Becoming a champion is not just a matter of having a big heart; it is also, perhaps even to a larger degree, a matter of intelligence. Please be smart about your training and your life. I genuinely care about you and want you to be healthy, and this is the same advice that I would give my own children. If you are fearful of some sort of serious injury, please walk away and come back to it later. The nice thing about personal challenges is that they are yours to own, and as such, they will always be there waiting for you. There is no need to rush, especially when there is an increased risk of getting hurt.

Predetermined commitments are a very focused and powerful form of concentration, and I believe that everyone has this capability. As is the case with many things however, your reward will be directly equal to the amount of effort that you put into the pursuit. I certainly understand that you probably aren't preparing to set a world record, but the message still applies. You can do incredible things, and you can absolutely overcome whatever is pulling you away from becoming your best. You can quit smoking. You can lower your cholesterol. You can lose that stubborn twenty pounds. You don't have to set records to be a champion. You have to win the fight against yourself to become a champion. You aren't competing against others, so don't become distracted by those that would like to keep you from your best. Your biggest battle is in taming your own mind and body, and that is something that you can do. There is a lot that goes into defeating your personal problems or achieving your personal bests, and I know that, but making up your mind to succeed no matter what is a great place to start. In the end, you have to commit yourself to your goal before you get tested. Success, I believe, begins in the mind, and we have all heard the expression that you have to first see it before you can get it. But that doesn't mean that we should negate the price that must be paid for achievement. Understanding what you are in for is vital to the endurance of the associated pain of victory. Enjoy it too, because if managed well, the price helps to separate you from all the others that failed. Today is a brand new day, and with it, can come a brand new start to your life. Live with a predetermined commitment to pursue only the best and overcome those obstacles that would have stopped you before. You weren't created by God to ultimately lose, so don't buy into the popular culture of failure and apathy. You were, however, created to be something special and something unique. Start your new life with a new purpose, and live in a way that twenty years from now you will be proud to speak of!

Affirmations:

1) I will commit myself to the success of the day before the difficulties of the journey begin.
2) Today I will lock my focus onto those things that deserve my attention while avoiding the distractions of those that don't.
3) I am tough, strong, durable, and able. Today, I win!

CHAPTER 11

Watch Your Language

That's an 18 year old me down South of the Border. I learned
more than I can write about from both the experience and
from the team psychologist that traveled with us.

In the late 1980s, I was competing in South America and had injured my
knee on my second attempt clean and jerk. As I sat back in the warmup
room waiting to be called for my last attempt, our US Team psychologist
came over to ask me how I felt. I replied, "Good," and with a smile I
continued with, "I never give up." He chuckled and then said, let's talk
later tonight." Never giving it a second thought, and when told by my
lifting coach that it was time, I proceeded to head out for my last lift of
the international event. As good leaders do, the psychologist waited for the
right time to educate me.

Later that night after dinner, he popped into my hotel room and asked
if we could talk. I was a total sponge and tried to take advantage of every

opportunity to get better. I was especially interested in the workings of the mind and how to become mentally better at not just lifting, but with living as well. He told me to pay close attention to how I talk to myself. I was somewhat puzzled because I thought that I was the most positive member of the team, but as he continued, I soon realized what he was driving at. His lesson has served me well for years, and it still does.

Just as there are various levels of performance on the competitive platform of weightlifting and powerlifting, the same holds true for mental toughness and the ability to maintain a positive approach to life. He continued by saying that the phrase "Never give up," might actually be more negative than positive, because it implies that the inherent setting of the mind is negative and that it must be overcome to succeed. Never giving up might actually be sending the message that you are prone to quitting, and therefore must overcome that tendency. He never said that the expression was a poor choice, because, as he continued to explain, it in large part depends on the emotional context that the statement is being attached to. He basically had two main ideas that he wanted to share with me that night.

The first was that thoughts and emotions are almost always connected, and if I was going to reach the heights and attain the goals that I had set for myself, I would have to be very aware of my self talk and the feeling that I get when I do so. This applies to you, as well. The way that we converse with ourselves, either internally or orally and aloud, has a much greater impact on our lives than we think. That being the case, we have to speak well to ourselves. We have to train our central nervous system to work for us, and self talk is a manifestation of how well we have done this.

The second highlight was that champions have to pay attention to details. The better someone is at managing the fine tuning of his or her craft, the better the odds of attaining success, and that includes the words that we choose when we talk, either to ourselves or to another. Going back to the expression "Never give up," his question to me was, "How did you feel when you said it?" When I told him that I felt, "All right," he suggested that I find a different expression that would elicit a better emotional response. His idea was to replace "Never give up" with "I will fight." It took me awhile to see the subtle difference, but it eventually became very clear to me. Even though it is qualified by the word "never," the phrase "give up" still denotes negativity. His suggestion "I will fight," is one hundred percent positive. No qualifications are needed to make it right, it already is. Again, and I want to make this clear, the team psychologist was not telling me to avoid the use of that statement, but he was challenging it. He wanted to ensure that if I were to use wording such as this, I understood what I should be feeling when I did. More important to me though, was his point that if we are going to truly be the best that we can be, even the details of our words must be thought through and paid attention to.

As already stated in this book, every thought produces a physiological response, and I believe that it is safe to say that our words do as well. Join Trent and me in choosing to speak well. I know life is hard, but complaining without a solution only compounds the problem by reinforcing the negative neural pathways of your mind and central nervous system. Try paying closer attention to how you speak, both to yourself and to others as well. Write down several well thought out statements and carry them with you throughout the day. Take them out and recite them every half hour or so. Start changing the way that you talk to yourself, and you will probably start to change the way that you see yourself, as well as the world around you. Do what's right, treat others with strength and kindness, and we think that you will soon begin to see the world in a new, improved, and better way.

Affirmations:

1) Today I will only speak favorably of myself and others.
2) I will resist the temptation of gossiping about others and engaging in negative self talk.
3) My new path of life starts today, and it begins with how I speak to myself. Today I claim victory over both my present and my future.

CHAPTER 12

Three Lessons from the University of Alabama

This is what hard work can do. This was my sophomore
year at the University of Alabama.

Playing football for The University of Alabama taught me much, but of all the lessons learned, I think three stand out more than the others. The first is that success is never an accident. There may be a number of factors at play that are beyond your control, but you still have to be doing the right things at the right time to be ready for those opportunities when they come. Success is a matter of preparation.

Those that prepare the most are much more likely to win, and that's a benefit because you have control over the amount of work that you put forth. We always had a top ranked team, but most were never aware of the amount of work that went into making this happen. Summer training camps were extremely difficult, and the threat of dehydration and its many complications were always looming. But the physical components of this preparation were just the beginning. We also had a responsibility to each other to know our jobs. Football is a team game, and the possibility of success is greatly limited by any weakness within the unit. In other words, the team will only be as strong as the weakest player, and that necessitates a lot of choreographed work. On the field, success only comes when everyone functions together, and that connects to life off of the field as well. For any of us to be dependable, we need to be at our best, and preparation is one of the keys to that.

The second most important thing that I took away from my days at Alabama was to never give up. It is impossible to succeed if you quit. Those hot summer sessions in the heat of the day down south would test anyone's mental and physical toughness. Those types of workouts make it easy to start thinking about what life would be like without football. Those sessions make it very easy to quit and give up, but to do so is to erase the possibility of great future things. Life is filled with difficulties and pains, and there is no escaping them, whether we quit or not. That being the case, we may as well get a reward from the struggles and fights. Giving up negates any possibility of that happening. One of our major goals for writing this book is to inspire you stay in the fight. Sometimes, you can't tell just how much further you have to go before that magical moment of victory is attained, and you never will if you give in to your desire for an easier path. The world is filled with people who wish they had tried and with those who wished they had tried a little longer. Don't live your life in the zone of regret. Stay the course and continue. Great days are ahead!

Last but not least is the idea that you have to get back up when you've been knocked down. Everyone fails, and that's all right. In fact, we think it's good. I think there is an expression that goes something like this: You can't tell how far you can go until you have first found out how far you can't go. Neither Bill nor I are sure who said that, but we both believe it's true. Failure teaches us many things, not the least of which is perseverance, the ability to keep at it when things seem at their worst. Football reinforces this idea exceptionally well because you won't score every time you have the ball, and you won't stop the other team from scoring every time they have it either. Getting knocked down mentally, physically, and/or emotionally, is an inherent part of the game, and that forces those that play it at that level to be that much stronger in those areas of life. But you don't have to be an all-star athlete to be in control of your thoughts and emotions, and our prayer is that you will take our lessons, adapt them to your own needs and wants, and take off. We know that you have the potential to break through the present barriers in your life and become that person that you dream of. Prepare, never give up, and stay the course. You are destined to be great!

Affirmations:

1) Champions get up after life has knocked them down. Today I will stand as a champion!
2) Today, before I even get started, I am going to prepare for the events of the day. Nothing will catch me off guard.
3) My actions dictate my progress. Today, I will act with the confidence of one who has already been to the top of life's mountain

Getting graded on every play can be difficult. The
mind has to be tougher than the body!

CHAPTER 13

Three Lessons from the Biggest Loser

Here I am on the ranch of The Biggest Loser.

Being on NBC's reality TV show The Biggest Loser was an incredible experience, and it opened many doors for me. It helped create a path for me to open my own gym called The Training for Life Facility, allowed me to land a number of speaking engagements, which I still do to this day, and form several business partnerships as well. But of all the things that I came away with from my time on the show, the most important lessons were those that can't be seen on the bottom line of a revenue ledger, and there were three of them.

The importance of incorporating proper nutrition into your lifestyle is more important than I can truly emphasize. The media does a great job of focusing on the negative effects of things like cigarettes, caffeine and alcohol, and too much sugar. They get an "A" for telling us what not to do, but they don't do nearly as well of a job with informing people about what they should be eating and drinking. Nutritional needs are highly dependent upon an individual's lifestyle. In other words, a professional athlete might require a much greater of amount of water intake when compared to a non-athlete. That being the case, a thorough discussion of nutrition is beyond the means of this book. What I can tell you is that what you put in your mouth directly affects your ability to perform and function. If your goal is to be the very best that you can be, then you need to become very much aware of that part of your life. Success is often hidden in the details, and nutrition is one of those.

Another very important thing that I took away from the show is that we have to make time for ourselves. Successful people tend to have very similar formulas for getting there. They all tend to be very driven, determined, and focused people, but when taken to the extreme for too long a period, breakdowns can occur. My co-author Bill, a multi-world record holder and champion draws and paints when not training and working on business projects. I enjoy yoga and walking. The point is that we must be balanced! Finding some time for yourself is vitally important for reenergizing both your body and mind. Those that maintain a high level of success for great lengths of time typically have a good number of interests beyond those of their chosen career path. Our advice to you is to investigate your interests outside of your "job." Look for a few things to do that you find relaxing and that give back to your quality of life in a way that is different from the others. Look for things that can add another dimension to your life.

The third thing that I think everyone should do is "find their why." I know that phrase is somewhat of a cliché, but your why will help to determine your level of success. Winning a pee wee football championship, although very important to those that experienced the accomplishment, is relatively easy when compared to winning the Rose Bowl. There is a much greater level of competition at the division one level of sports, and that usually brings with it a much greater level of commitment by those athletes that play in it. If "your why," which is really another way of expressing the reasons for your choosing to do something, is superficial in nature, you won't have the type of commitment necessary to stay on top. For the most part, and if you plan on being highly successful, you have to have a fundamental love and passion for what you are doing. The greater the love and passion, the less superficial your desire will be, and it is often that desire that separates those that make it from those that don't. The more I write about this, the clearer it becomes that "your why" is equivalent to the level of your desire. Start asking yourself why you are choosing to do what you are. Ask yourself where you want to go with it, and then see if your level of desire matches the level of success you are envisioning. If all thumbs are up, start the process today. If your desire doesn't line up with your goals, either change one so that they do meet, or start looking for another "why." Investigate the potential of your life and you will soon start realizing how much you have to develop and offer the world.

Affirmations:

1) Today I will take time to reenergize. I will spend time with those that I love and with the things that I love to do.
2) Today I will recognize that I am of little use to others if I have not taken care of myself. Today, I will make those around me better by making myself better.
3) Today I will look deeper into why I am doing what I do. I will find a bigger and better sense of purpose in my job, and with all that I choose to engage in.

Here's a photo of me in high school. I was recruited
by colleges to throw the shot as well.

PART THREE

Paying it Forward

Whether we are talking about becoming a division one college football player at the University of Alabama and winning bowl games or setting world records and winning international championships in powerlifting, both require the right type of dedicated lifestyle. A person's way of life is really nothing more than a series of choices, and they can either add up to be good or bad. The choices that Trent and I made throughout our respective athletic careers served us wonderfully well, but perhaps even more important is the fact that they continue to do so even today. As our individual lives continue to move forward, we recognize just how important our pasts were. Our decisions to be committed, disciplined, faithful, and to walk away from temptation helped to pave the way for many successes, and they still do.

Although the final section of *Lifting Spirits; World Champion Advice for Everyday Living* contains essays referring back to our competitive days, it still remains true to the original concept of the book. Our main goals were for you to believe that you could reach new heights in your life, become a better and more productive you, and to live the type of life that you would be proud to call your own, and that hasn't changed. There is one addition, however. What we noticed as we did our own motivational speeches and seminars was that when we helped others, we helped ourselves. Consistent with that last thought, there are basically three groups of people in this world.

At the bottom of the list are those that have no desire to serve anyone but themselves. This is the group that you would do best to stay away from. In the middle are those that do the right thing, but not necessarily for the right reasons. These people are motivated, but not always trustworthy. They have a tendency to change their principles and ethics when it suits them best, and this makes them unreliable. The third group does the right thing for the right reasons. These people recognize the greater good and will give of themselves to make the team as a whole operate more efficiently. These people are the most dependable, and they are always looking for the win-win situation.

Athletes, on the other hand, are trained to defeat the opposition. There is no win-win in the mindset of elite level competitors. There is an honor system, and there's mutual respect, but no win-win. And that is probably the biggest transformation in the lives of both Trent and myself. As champions, our job was to eliminate those opposing us, where as now, as retired champions, we look to help everyone that we can. As competitors, we kept secrets, but as authors, we share them.

In this last section, we give some of the advice that we believe will help you to see the world in a unique way. Again, this is the same life-coaching advice that we give to those who hear us speak, as well as to our own children. I suppose that there is a potentially different percentage for everyone, but I think we can agree that to a large extent the world exists in our perceptions of it. In other words, the world that you see and relate to is mostly created in your own mind. In part, this is why some people smile during a thunderstorm and others hide under the bed. Our final goal is to pay our version of the world forward to you. I know it's been said before, but this is the first day of the rest of your life. Positive and happy people live longer and more productive lives, and as of now, consider yourself part of that fraternity. When you are strong, you can afford to be kind and benevolent, and if you are not yet there, start developing yourself today so that you can be tomorrow. Walk out your door and greet the world with a determined smile. Look for opportunities to help those in need. As you'll see in the upcoming essays, there are a number of ways do this. Be creative and think outside of the examples that we have shared. We think that you'll agree that when you pay forward your good fortunes, you'll get back more than you gave.

In the end, Trent and I have come to believe that success is much more a way of life than it is a series of temporary accomplishments. Gold medals are nice, but the lifespan of the events themselves are quite temporary. Compared to world championship victories and college bowl games won, we think that a much better measurement of success is what one does for others. Surely no medal can honor such behavior, but helping your fellow brother or sister carriers its own rewards, and you can be assured that they last much longer. If you are really blessed, you can do both! We believe in your potential. If you can chase down and capture your dreams while helping others along the way, you will be able to call yourself a champion of life, and that's becoming increasingly rare. Pursue the very best in all aspects of your being, and join the few who help to make the world a better place. One person might not be able to change the world, but he or she might be able to change a part of it. If enough of us chip in, the possibilities become virtually limitless. Pay your success forward and start the reaction today!

Affirmations:

1) Today I will look for ways to make the world a better place.
2) Today I will think a lot less about what can go wrong and a lot more about can go right.
3) Today I will not only make myself better, but I will look for opportunities to make someone else better too.

CHAPTER 14

Heroes

Several years ago, I was rewarded by a local police department for helping to save a man's life. For a number of rather obvious reasons, I was both grateful and humbled by the honor, but it made me think about what actually defines a hero. And although I was named one the day of the ceremony, I questioned whether I truly deserved such a bestowment. Before I move forward on my thoughts of heroism, I would like to describe the events of the day, because to me, they further support the notion that many things happen to us for a reason and that we have a direct line to a higher and guiding power.

While driving to the store, I pulled up to a potentially deadly scene, but I wasn't supposed to be where I ended up, and no one will ever be able to convince me that this was a coincidence. I'll let you draw your own conclusions, but here is the account of what happened on this June afternoon. On a typical day following work, my job was to get to the gym and train, then be home by 6 PM for dinner with the family. On this day, however, I was grading state tests and was running late. To make matters worse, my wife called and needed me to stop at the afore-mentioned store before heading to my workout. Not only did that dramatically change my arrival time to the gym, but it also forced me to take a route that I never would have otherwise used. Driving around the curve leading to the overpass that was needed to get to the grocery store, I noticed a number of cars stopped, and a group of people in the street looking at something. Realizing that whatever it was wasn't good, I slowed my speed. It did not take long for me to see a very large man overpowering a police officer. I estimate the man to have been somewhere around 6"4' in height and weighing in excess of 300 pounds. The officer was obviously compromised, but no one was helping him. I jumped out from my car, and ran toward the fight. The policeman saw me, and yelled, "Help!" Without going into needless details, the man was subdued, placed into handcuffs, and taken away. The police officer that day was a real hero. Everyday, people like him selflessly risk their lives to help those in need, and that giant of a guy fit into that classification well. I didn't know this at the time, but he had escaped from a local mental institution and was attempting to commit suicide by jumping from the bridge. The officer was driving by, happened to see this, and stepped in to stop the sure death! In fact, he didn't even have time to notify other officers of what was happening, or what he was doing, because if he had, it would have been, ostensibly, too late. I was proud to be able to assist him that day, but many heroes don't wear uniforms, and most will never come across the chance to rush into a burning building and rescue the little child that would otherwise perish in flames! Now, there is no doubt in my mind that the policeman was a hero, but as we talked after the event had ended, he referred to me as one too. I wasn't so sure.

When I questioned myself about whether or not I deserved that title, my thoughts and beliefs were that I didn't. To be honest, I actually called the police department and told them that I really didn't deserve what they wanted to do for me. I continued to think that way even after I spoke to a different officer on the phone that had asked me if I had noticed how many cars had pulled over. I knew the answer, and then I quickly realized the direction in which he was heading. Although many had stopped, they did so to watch, not to help. For the record, two other civilians came to assist as well. One lady informed us that she had called the police for further backup, and another man stepped in toward the end of the incident, although I am more than confident that he would have gotten involved earlier had he come across the situation sooner. Following our conversation, I still wasn't convinced that I was hero, but I did change my mind about attending the ceremony. The struggle to define this concept continued in my brain, and I began looking back at and analyzing other events in my life. Additionally, I wondered if I had been in the midst of heroes in the past, and if so, how often?

When I was 15 years old, I competed at the New York State Championships, and back then, there were no age groups, or divisions of any kind, other than by weight. In other words, I was competing as a kid against men in their twenties and thirties. Things have since changed for the better, but those days taught me very valuable lessons, some of which are included in this book. Anyway and in an attempt to keep up with the big guys, I chose to lift a weight that I really had no business trying. In the sport of weightlifting, an athlete is given a total of three attempts, and I missed all three of mine. This disqualified me from the event, and I was dejected. It was a hot summer day in Buffalo, and I sat outside the venue, alone, fighting back my emotions. A few moments later, a medic sat down beside me with the offer of an icepack and drink. He took a few minutes to talk to me, and although I wasn't ready to speak back, I did listen. His words helped to shift both my state of mind and emotion. He was not under any obligation to comfort me, and a person of less sensitivity would have failed to recognize the opportunity at hand, but he took full advantage of the situation and changed the course of that day! He saw an individual in need, and took action. I remember him saying, "Anyone that cares this much about their sport is bound to go far. I'm a big fan of weightlifting because I have a bad back, and can't do it. One day, I'm going to see your picture in the magazines!" At that instant, and I mean this with total sincerity, I felt hope and became encouraged. I am well aware that the medic that day certainly didn't fit into the traditional framework of what we see in our minds when the word hero is mentioned, but if heroes help people in times of need, he certainly performed as one. He may not have charged into a burning building or dodged bullets to rescue otherwise helpless victims, nor were his words poetic, speech worthy, or prophetic, but he did make a profound impact on my life. His kindness gave me the emotional and psychological lifts that were needed for me to see the future of tomorrow beyond where I was at that moment, and that was powerful. I speak of this often, but seeing through the eyes of faith is vital to rising out of the depths of one's despair. You probably won't get to better days without a plan or metaphorical map, and the eyes of faith serve that purpose extraordinarily well. The more I thought about this, the more I began to classify him as a hero! If kindly chosen words, conviction, and a desire to help constituted his being one, then there must have been others as well.

When I was in my late thirties and a teacher, I received a moment-defining letter in the mail. I remember the letter day well because it was written by a former student of mine who wanted to say "Thanks!" The events of what happened here are sort of reversed and confusing, so I'm going to start from the beginning.

It was a rainy day in April, and I was sick with a terrible cold. I couldn't wait to go home. At the work day's end, I was walking towards the exit at the end of the hall when I saw a student of mine looking out of sorts. She wasn't presently crying, but it was clear that she had been. The last thing I wanted to do was stop and discuss someone else's problems because they were almost always typical teenage things that, although important to them, were still trivial in the bigger scheme of life. When I became a teacher however, I made a promise (to myself) that I would always put my students ahead of me, and I have always chosen to honor that. I thank the Lord that I did. I asked if she was all right, and she said, "Yes." Her body language, face, and eyes made it abundantly clear, however, that she was lying. I gently pressed, and she confessed that she needed to talk to someone. As we spoke in the hallway, I began to understand that this was no minor or ordinary issue and that this poor girl was at the idiomatic end of her rope. Things were happening in this child's life that went beyond what anyone should have to deal with, and the police needed to be brought in. I was fortunate on two counts. First, she trusted me, and secondly, one of my good friends, Deputy Bob Stapleton from The Sheriff's Office, was still working. He agreed to stop at the school and help us out, and he did so with the compassion of a true humanitarian. Bob knew exactly what to do and how to do it. My work day officially ended at 3 PM, but I didn't get home until well after five. It took some time for the implemented solutions to affect the necessary changes, but everything worked out for her, and to my knowledge, she continues to do well. During the time of her crisis, the young lady was a senior in high school heading towards graduation. Happily, she finished the academic year with strength and walked across the stage to get her diploma. There was something however that she neglected to tell me until I opened that letter sent through the mail. She had informed Deputy Stapleton and me of a number of things that day in April, but she never mentioned suicide. As I read her letter, I began to realize the magnitude of what Deputy Stapleton and I had done that day. She went on to say that she was planning to take her own life, and the fact that I stopped and spent time with her showed that some people do genuinely care. I suppose that on some level we gave her hope, and sometimes that's all people need. For those of you reading that are fighting against what appear to be overwhelming odds: depression, anxiety, despair, and other things of the like, please remember that there is always hope. Just because you haven't found the solution to the problems you are facing does not mean that they don't exist. You may have to look outside of yourself to find them, but they are there. Talk to someone whom you can trust, someone that can provide clear and strategic guidance. Oftentimes and in the midst of our problems, we are too emotionally involved to think in terms of positive outcomes, but other people can. As long as you are around to see the next morning's light, there is always the opportunity for change, and with that comes the potential for a better day. We always have choices. You can make it out of the darkness and into the light. Choose to be solution oriented! Choose to be kind, tough, and to endure! Choose victory! Choose life!

After all of this, and although I'm getting closer, I am still not sure of how to exactly define the concept of what a hero is, but I have definitely learned two things from trying to figure it out. The first is that it is a much bigger concept, at least in my mind, than initially meets the eye. As such, the number of adjectives needed to successfully pin down an accurate definition is just too broad to do so. Secondly, I may not necessarily be able to define the word hero, but I know one when I see one. The medic that I wrote about earlier is a hero. Two of my middle school teachers who guided me through very difficult times, Mr. Greg Stanton and Mr. Larry Bucchioni are heroes. In fact, I think that we have many heroes in society, and they usually don't wear tights or have capes draped from their necks and shoulders. Police officers and firefighters are always included in the conversation, but it needs to be expanded to those teachers, social workers, and others of the like that selflessly give of themselves for the benefit of others. If you are one of these people, consider yourself included into this fraternity! I was fortunate in that I received a letter of thanks letting me know how I had helped, but many never get this. Either way, be assured that you are appreciated. In fact, and on behalf of those who never got around to acknowledging you, I will. Thank you for being who you are and for doing what you do! You are helping to make the world a better place, so keep at it.

In the end, defining the word hero isn't nearly as important as living it, and you, the reader, have the power to help change the course of someone's life. Look for opportunities to help. A simple smile and a "hello" might mean more than you think to a child, man, or woman in need. One person can make a difference. Lead by example, be kind, and be a hero!

Affirmations:

1) Today I will speak the language of victory to someone who needs it most.
2) Today I will recognize that the only way to maintain the outside is to first focus on the inside.
3) Today I will give more of myself so that others can have a little more of themselves.

CHAPTER 15

By Invitation Only

One of our local schools runs a yearly Wellness Day. Classes of about 20 students at a time enter to see various presentations. My discussion revolves around how great the future can be if the right choices are made. I also bend steel, roll up commercial grade frying pans, and tear decks of poker cards with my bare hands. The kids seem to like it!

The most important house you will ever invest in is the one between your ears. Houses provide us with a place to live, sleep, rest, eat, and so on. But they are also units of storage. Almost everything that we own gets accumulated and kept in our houses, and our minds are very similar. The major difference between the two is in what gets held on to. The house saves clothing, furniture, and other assorted articles, but the mind stores infinitely more valuable commodities. The contents of the mind determine moods, emotions, and invariably, the course of one's life. It's doubtful that you would let just anyone into your personal home. If the mind is your gateway to success, failure, and the paradigms of life that get created, why would you allow just anyone or anything into it? The problem is that most of us don't think along these lines, but that doesn't negate the concept's authenticity or value. I assure you that filtering your inputs can have a very positive and profound impact on your life, and hopefully, the following will illustrate this well.

Everything that we watch, listen to, and engage in creates thoughts, and those thoughts generate neural pathways that illicit a physiological response. In other words, what we think about manifests itself in physical ways. The mind and the body are very much connected. For years, athletes knew this, but they couldn't prove it. Thanks in part to technological advancements, however, we now can. Brain imaging reveals that every thought, every psychological action, yields a physiological reply, and that is fundamentally important to both know and remember. This is especially true for those on a path to become the very best versions of themselves possible. I'm not an expert in this field, so please do your own research, but I am quite confident that what I am sharing is accurate. If you have doubts about the mind/body connection, stop and think about the last time you had a nightmare. My guess is that prior to your dream you were resting very comfortably in bed. Physically, everything was fine. That is, until the fears kicked in. Once the nightmare began, your pulse and blood pressure rose, your respirations increased, and depending on its severity, you may have even started sweating. But, the dream wasn't real; it was imagined, and it was all in your head. Of paramount importance here is that your body reacted as though it were real, and that is because your subconscious mind cannot tell the difference between reality and fiction. The point is that the mind and the body are attached, and we need to look no further than our own experiences to prove it.

It is clear that what we eat, drink, and put into our bodies directly affects our physical well-being. I am going to suggest that what you watch, listen to, and otherwise put into your head, is equally as significant. Because most people will never have the opportunity to immediately see the results of their thoughts on a screen, or receive test results on paper, they dismiss the importance of thought training. That said, it's a difficult task to persuade many people on this topic. Conversely, athletes almost always get it. They have lived it, and they know what it's like to be in the "zone." They also know what it's like to be out of it. When I conduct seminars and give my motivational talks to teams, they routinely share their experiences on how thoughts both precipitated and influenced outcomes, and the same is true for all of us, athletes or not.

A couple of years ago, I received a phone call from a former student asking if I would be willing to be a reference for her. She was a nice young lady, filled with potential too, so I agreed. She began telling me how she had an upcoming interview scheduled and how she was trying to get prepared. She never asked for advice, so I didn't offer any. I just listened. It's been awhile since this conversation, but I distinctly recall her stating, at least a handful of times, that she probably wouldn't get the job. And she was right; she didn't. She called me back a few weeks later, and I asked her if she was surprised that she didn't get it. She said "No," but what did surprise her was when I said, "Neither am I." I explained to her that the language of the past conversation was self-defeating, and she confessed that although she didn't remember saying she wouldn't get the job, she did feel very negative about her overall prospects. At that point, I became very interested as to where this negativity had come from because she had never seemed to be fundamentally pessimistic in the past. Turns out, she had just recently moved in with two new roommates. Unfortunately, they didn't see the world in the same way that she did. Both roomies were heavy partiers, and they tended to be negative and sarcastic, not only with each other and with life in general, but with her as well. While my former student tried to prepare for her interview, the other girls would attempt to sabotage her by turning up the volume of music and by telling her that "she wasn't pretty enough to land a gig like that." For whatever reason, my former student, Kim, took those words to heart and they very unfortunately impacted the outcome of the interview. Our brains are constantly creating the pathways that I spoke of earlier. They are similar to roads in that the more you travel on them, the easier it gets to travel on them again. These "roadways" become ingrained into the central nervous system's memory, and the response becomes more automatic. Basically, those two roommates, in a very short amount of time, had trained Kim's brain to fail, and she did. They had trained her to become a negative thinker. My advice to her was to get out of that situation because who we hang around is often times who we become. If you want to spiral downhill, go make friends and spend a lot of time with thieves, thugs, liars, and others of that type of fabric. It won't be long, and you'll be at the bottom too. The good news is that it can work the other way as well.

I say the following with all humility because it was the Lord Jesus Christ that guided me along the path of my lifting career. I never controlled the timing of the events that occurred, so I would be a liar and a fool to profess that I got where I did alone. It's actually quite the opposite; I got where I did despite my inadequacies, and I thank God Almighty for that! Having said this, my results suggested that I was an elite strength athlete, but my game didn't reach its peak until I began spending time with those that were legends in the sport. I didn't win my first world title until I started surrounding myself with other world champions, and that was no coincidence. Where my thoughts went, my performance followed, but it was who I was connecting myself to that helped to form those all important mental frameworks and propel me to a level that I had never previously attained. The grey matter is much deeper than what I have just chronicled however, and I wonder if we know more about the depths of the oceans than we do about the recesses of our own minds.

Throughout my years as a teacher, I have coached many lifters, some through school and some out of the confines of the district. One in particular was a strong, tough, and hungry kid. Because he had numerous home related issues and problems like I did when I was around that age, he kind of reminded me a little of myself. In any event, I began to notice some changes in his mood, and he started entering his training sessions very fatigued. My first thought was that he had fallen victim to drug use, but that was soon ruled out, so we continued to problem solve. He was having a very difficult time sleeping and complained of feeling very negative (but not necessarily depressed). Strangely, everything in his life seemed to be all right, or at least better than what it had been in the past, but his lifting results soon began to drop, and we were both somewhat confused. I took him out to eat after a training session, and his conversation began to reveal a few things. He quickly showed that he was preoccupied with the topics of mutilation, torture, and death. Quite honestly, I felt a little weirded out. To be clear, he wasn't condoning, supporting, or endorsing such things; he was just talking about them from the perspective that he too was weirded out. On top of that, I was also confused, and my lack of understanding led to a series of questions. This is where it became very interesting. I asked him to explain any new things in his life that were not in the picture before he started his downward spiral. In other words, I was trying to figure out what could be the cause of such a dramatic shift in attitude. Eventually we found that he had just been introduced to a new "musical band" in the genre of black/death metal. He would put his ear buds in and then go to sleep every night listening to the lyrics included in the music. He had been doing this for several weeks, and those messages kept playing in his head over and over. I am well aware that people listen to this stuff all the time and never become killers or violent criminals. I get that! I am also very well aware of the argument that this type of "art" doesn't have a negative impact on those who listen to it. I try not to judge with a broad brush, and I'm not going to start here. What I will say is that it definitely affected this young man, and I think it did because he was trying to reach levels that he had never been able to attain before. If your measure of performance is significantly lower than your level of talent, the ramifications and details of your choices won't reveal themselves. To make this point a little clearer, I'll put it into the form of an analogy. If you are good enough to play major league baseball, and you are scheduled to play against a middle school team, smoking and drinking the night before probably won't cause your performance to *appear* any worse, but it would be. To bring this home, now think about trying to engage in the smoking and drinking the night before lifestyle and then playing against a group of major league equals. Do you see the difference and subsequent point? My lifter's choice of entertainment hurt him, and it showed, but only because he was competing against his previous best. He was trying to reach those new performance heights and quickly found out that even the smallest of choices made had a profound impact. If he were satisfied with competing at 70% of his best, then the margin of error would have been on his side, and the effects of his choices wouldn't have been seen. But not being seen and not existing are two very different things. Because the included lyrics in those songs directly opposed his convictions and values, they created a conflict within his own mind, and any unresolved battle will consume energy. His choice of music would have affected him, it's just that no one would have known. The point I'm trying to make is this; If you are attempting to do the types of things that others can only dream of, you will have to pay attention to the smallest of details in life and then make choices in such a way as to maximize your efforts while minimizing any damages. The desire that it takes to reach your standards has to be at least equal to the effort that it will take to get there. It is a very disciplined lifestyle, and very few will actually maintain it for any great length of time, *but you have the potential to be the exception*!

I'm not suggesting that you never watch the news or tune in to what the media offers, but I am telling you that it is impossible to feel good when you are allowing your psyche to be bombed by negativity. After we discovered what was at the root of his depression, he began to turn things around, both mentally and physically. It wasn't long, and he was back to himself. Just as importantly, this anecdote helps to illustrate the power of the mind. How many times have you unknowingly walked around all day singing the same song over and over in your head? Hopefully, all of your inputs have uplifting and positive messages attached to them. Whether you are pursuing world and national powerlifting titles or the career of your dreams, the victory is hidden in the details of your choices made. Train your mind well, or it will train you!

Finally, please realize that what's important is not only who you surround yourself with, but what you surround yourself with as well. As far as I am concerned, you are personally inviting into your home whatever it is on the TV and ipod that you are watching and listening to, so be cautious. Everyday brings with it the opportunity for new and better success. Inviting only the best into your mental home is a great place to start!

Affirmations:

1) Today I will be aware of what I am watching and listening to and make sound decisions as to what I allow into my head.
2) Today I will surround myself with as many positive people I can.
3) Today I will actively delete all the negatives that attempt to enter into my brain by consciously choosing not to focus and dwell on them.

CHAPTER 16

Badly Wrapped Gifts

Here is the "first family of powerlifting;" the Bucchionis!
From left to right; Maria, Josh, and Larry.

At some point, death comes for us all, and although it may sound strange, there are many hidden positives in this. Not to be comical, but without some framework of time as a reference, I don't know what we would ever accomplish. Think about it. There would be a total lack of urgency to do anything, because without death, there would always be another tomorrow. It would lead to the ultimate in procrastination, and the Lord knows that many of us don't need another excuse to put off until tomorrow what we could do today. The truth is, provided that you are willing to look at your own mortality, there may be no other factor as motivating as death to get one immediately started on a new course of life. These are all mute points however, because we know for a fact that death will come. Tomorrow is not guaranteed to any us, and that's one of the ultimate truths. When we get right down to it, and you may have heard this before, "We don't beat death by living longer, we beat death by living better!" The preceding statement may be somewhat cliché, but it is nonetheless accurate. None of us knows what lies ahead, so we had better take care of business today.

Fellow Strength Hall of Famers, Larry and Maria Bucchioni exemplify this as well as anyone I have ever met. Their story is unique and one that ought to instill within us a fire of motivation, purpose, and drive like none other. The Bucchionis, in the face of the worst possible scenarios that life can throw at us, pushed forward, stayed the course of faith, and persevered. In many ways, they left behind a path, a clearly cut trail, for all those warriors of honor to follow. They exemplify the words character, grit, and champion! Ironically, I would not be able to label them with such great praise if it weren't for what they had to go through. To the victor, adversity and opportunity are synonymous. Before getting to the details of their life together, I need to elaborate on this point, because in large part, it provided the inspiration behind this writing.

The other day, I was watching the Spiderman movie, and some observations floated into my otherwise empty head. The great character of Spiderman could not possibly exist without an equally great, although evil, oppositional force. Without the Green Goblin, there would be no need for a Spiderman. Without the Joker, Batman serves no purpose. Superheroes would not be able to save the day if they had no evil force to fight against. The opportunities to take a stand for what is right, kind, true, and just are often found in the struggle against hate, anger, and immorality. Similarly, the opportunities for greatness and strength are often concealed within the struggle against what appears to be overwhelming odds and weakness. Additionally, the greater your goals, the more difficult the opposition will be. Even though there are many similarities between the two, I think that winning a state championship is much easier than winning the worlds, and I believe that most would agree. Oppositions though, can come in many forms and variations, some of which we choose and some of which we don't.

Maria Bucchioni never chose her greatest adversary, and it came in the form of a rare cancer. You have no doubt noticed that in the second paragraph I referred to Maria in the present tense, and I did so for a very good reason. Even though the great Mrs. Bucchioni has moved on, her legacy continues to drive forward and inspire. Her type of greatness is not the kind that can be erased. Maria was a pioneer in the field of women's powerlifting. She was a national champion and record holder, teacher, friend, mother, and wife, and she did all of this in spite of what she was up against. I remember Larry, her loyal husband and colleague in strength, telling me that she would come home from her treatments, repetitively throw up, and then head down to the gym to train. That's toughness. Now, to do what she did might not have been super-human, but it sure was super-hero! The way in which Maria handled the adversity dealt to her is worthy of a king's, or in this case, a queen's highest praise. Champions have a way of doing what is right even when what they are facing is blatantly wrong, and no one did this better than she (or Larry). There is a fundamental difference between just being alive and really living. Maria understood that, and she acted accordingly.

On one particular occasion, Maria, after being told that the cancer had spread to her liver, went through a bone-marrow transplant followed by chemotherapy. The following day, she and Larry drove to Glenns Falls, NY for a competition. Maria won best female lifter! The physical power required to pull this off must have been incredible, but I am so much more impressed, however, with the mental and emotional strength needed. Nearly everyone would have gone into a deep state of despair following the unfortunate medical news, but Maria seemed to get stronger. It's a marvel, and it affectively shows what we are truly capable of when we are totally committed.

To accomplish what she did, under the circumstances that she faced, is really quite remarkable. You cannot overcome what you won't face. Maria Bucchioni confronted and responded to her challenges with the spirit, determination, courage, honor, and faith of a true warrior! In my mind, Maria Bucchioni never lost a fight to cancer. She carried out her mission as outlined and directed by God, and she did it, dare I say, as near to perfect as can be. She has won, and no disease can defeat the example of how to live well set forth by Maria Bucchioni! Larry Bucchioni's story and role in his wife's life is of no less value.

Larry is a multi world champion and world record holder, and he continues to compete in the master's divisions at an incredible age of near 70. In fact, he still deadlifts well in excess of 500 pounds, again, at the age of nearly 70. This story, however, is not about winning on the platform or in the competitive environment, it's about winning in life. Larry, much as his wife did, has pressed on through the hardest of times, made it through the rain, and found both happiness and success.

Not too long ago, I visited the child's sick ward at a local hospital. A friend of mine thought that the kids would like to see me bend some steel bars, roll up some frying pans, and perform a couple of other strongman stunts. When finished, I talked with one of the doctors there. I asked him what he felt were the most important things needed for recovery. He told me in one word, "support." I immediately thought of Larry Bucchioni. Larry, although in a different manner and role, was just as much of a champion as his misses. When it came to being a source of strength for his wife, and being the rock of support that we all look for, no one could have done the job better than he. During this dark period, Mr. Bucchioni was teaching at Susquehanna Valley Central Schools, coaching the varsity football team, raising his young son, and caring for and training with his wife. Often times, Larry would train at around midnight. After all the events of the day, many of them mentally and emotionally draining, he still found and made time for pursuit of success. If you are a person that wants to work out and get healthier, but claims there isn't time, I suggest you restructure your thinking. I also suggest that you restructure your schedule as well. There's time, provided that you both look for it and then prioritize accordingly.

Larry has passed all of the necessary testing to be called champion, and again, I'm not referring to those titles earned in the arena of competition (Those are almost too numerous to keep track of). Larry and Maria Bucchioni are champions because they have given more to people than they may know. I hope and pray that neither I nor you, the reader, have to go through what they did, but it comforts me to know that it's possible to handle it in a manner consistent with a king's faith, attitude, and character. Every time we go through a crisis, or worse, we have the ability to provide the gift of leadership to those heading into, or already in, the eye of the storm. Someone somewhere is fighting something very similar to what we have already survived. Is there any better gift to give? Aside from forgiveness or true love, I know of none! A few years ago, a friend of mine went through a terrible ordeal, and he confessed that it brought him to his knees. As we talked, I reminded him of what Larry Bucchioni had faced, and overcome. A year later, and as we talked over dinner, he told me how important that reminder was. He realized that he wasn't alone. When we face hardships, difficulties, and tragedies, try to remember that we are blazing a trail for someone else to follow. Let's light a path for everyone to see and set an example for all. The Bucchionis did, and many are grateful!

Affirmations:

1) Understanding that tomorrow is never guaranteed, I will live today to its absolute fullest.
2) Today I will live in such a way as to set an example that I would want my most cherished of loved ones to follow.
3) Today I will live by allowing the fear of future regret to guide my choices and actions

CHAPTER 17

Waking Up

My coaches from York Barbell were the best anybody could have had. They led and taught by example, and I will always be thankful for my time with them!

The other day, the alarm went off and my first thought was, "This blows!" It was dark, cold, and I had a number of pressing things headed straight for me on this day, and my initial beliefs weren't doing me any favors. I have already written about why responses are superior to reactions, so I won't elaborate too much, but my response training quickly kicked in, and my perceptions began to shift and change. Through example, Dick Smith and Leo Totten, my former Olympic Weightlifting coaches and legends in the strength world, taught me the value of aggressively choosing the course for each day. As it applies here, aggressively choosing is antagonistic and oppositional to the more commonly implemented and passive approach.

The passive philosophy allows one to feel justified with his or her negative mentality. This type of person may not even be aware of the fact that he or she "woke up on the wrong side of the bed," or, maybe the individual is intuitive enough to notice a sour taste in the mouth, but hasn't changed the mind's concept, subsequent actions, or the result. These types of people are still in reaction mode, and reactions are inferior for a number of reasons, not the least of which is because they do not consider a plan of counter attack, or effective measure to change the course of the flow of negativity that is currently being experienced. Reactionary people assume that they can't control their own feelings. I understand that we do not control everything that happens to us, but we have total control over the way that we answer back. Reactionaries often surrender this ability. On top of that and often times, one bad event leads to a downward spiraling of thinking, and this continues until a more positive external event takes place, thus changing the paradigm within the mind of that person. The inherent problem is obvious in that these types of people are always at the mercy of "fate." On the other hand, a response driven person both recognizes and aggressively changes the negative emotional charge that is felt. Both types of people wake up with similar circumstances, but how they deal with them are fundamentally different. Recent data more than supports the notion that much of what we do is driven by emotions, and that should be reason enough for any semi-conscious person to want to be in the most optimal state of mind possible, but to do that requires that we be both aware and actively engaged.

Uplifting self talk is one of the cornerstones of response, and it is equally integral to emotional shifts. As opposed to giving in to the opening and pessimistic thoughts of the morning, I changed my focus to that of opportunity and excitement, by speaking, in my own mind, of what could go right with the day and reminding myself of the numbers of times that I had been victorious in moments much more serious and dramatic than those to be presented ahead.

Granted, I had some of the best coaches in the world to guide me through this process. However, and I know that I have stated this before, there was nothing special, in terms of inherent traits, about either them or me. Additionally, I can assure you that I was not exposed to this training of the mind until my high school years, and that meant that I had to overcome my already subconsciously and consciously patterned, programmed, and well-ingrained mental approaches to life, some of which were downright unproductive. Don't let anyone convince you that, for whatever reason, you can't do this. You may have to go see a specialist, and/or change your diet, and maybe even substantially amend your lifestyle and change who you keep company with, but I believe that it is possible to see the world in a different and more beneficial way. Your circumstances are changeable, and sometimes that transition starts within your own mind.

As I wrote about earlier and when I was quite young, several social workers routinely paraded in and out of my house attempting to figure out whether or not I should be removed and placed into foster care. The most memorable of these workers was a man named Brian, and I believe that he genuinely cared for me and wanted to do what was right. At one point, he flat out asked me if I would leave (and go to a foster home). My answer was that if I was forced, I would come back (to my mom) every time, and there would be no stopping me. I'm thankful that he listened, because some people don't. Frequently, during this period, I would buy much of my own food and attempt to do my own laundry and try to be of as much assistance to my mother as possible, so I understood why they were there, but that didn't change my views on their proposal. There, of course, was much more going on than just this, but the details aren't really that important. More so is the idea that a river of negativity had been flowing through my head for years, and the longer we spend ingraining those patterns only means the longer that it will take to re-route. Re-routing, though, is possible! To this day, I still wrestle with some of those demons that were created back in my youth, but I have them in a choke hold. They still fight back, but I always win, and to an extent, I'm actually thankful for them.

When the alarm rings, consider it an opportunity. Try changing the thought of "I have to" to "I get to!" You are fortunate to live in this nation with all of its benefits. The possibilities that you need for a better life surround you. Get out there and take advantage of them! Don't start your day passive, allowing the variables of how you wake up, or those of the day's future, to force you on a path of self-destruction. Wake up with a mission! As you prepare to rise, tell yourself, "This is my day, and I choose to take control of what I can!" "I am a champion, and I am going to carry myself with the dignity of one." I think I recall seeing a quote that says something like even before the moment that you spin around in bed to make contact with the floor, boldly affirm that the forces of darkness would do well to step aside. I know it's probably not written exactly like that, but I totally agree with the premise. I think better still, develop and write down your own affirmations. Have them in a place where you can read them at the day's first sight of eye, and make them meaningful too. If life is like your very own movie that you get to take control of, you may as well write a great script to go with it. Take control and write well!

Affirmations:

1) Today I will wake up with a mission, with a desire to see it completed, and a plan to get it done.
2) I will start my day with a vision of how I want it to end and then start working from there.
3) I will take today head on, looking for the opportunity in each challenge.

CHAPTER 18

It's too Late not to Start

Several members of the Strength and Power Hall of Fame. An incredible group of human beings. It's an honor to be in the same room with them! From left to right: Paul Dick, Rick Bucinell, Bill Clark, Larry Bucchioni, Don Reinhoudt, and Mark Krieger

During my seminars, I often speak of something called central nervous system response. In short, the CNS is responsible for encoding and memorizing responses to every stimulus that we become faced with. It is not so much the event itself that we face that determines whether we create a positive or negative neural pathway, but our perception of the event that matters the most. This is why what we think is so crucial to our well-being.

An optimistic person finds it is easier to think positively than a negative person because the upbeat one has ingrained more appropriate responses and they have become the default setting. Unfortunately, this works the same way, albeit in the opposite direction, for negative people. They have created so many pessimistic responses to events that the default setting for them has been set to negative. But being healthy is more than just thought related, it is physical too, and just like we create patterns of response for our thinking, we create the same physiologically.

Not too long ago, a high school friend Facebooked me and asked for some workout advice. This man has never been the vision of good health and has always, as far back as I can remember, been overweight. During our conversation, he mentioned to me that he was turning the corner to 50, and he needed to do something, or he felt as though he would be on the fast track to death. Then he said something that really caught my attention. With a big sigh he stated, "It's probably too late anyway." I don't have too much anger in me, but if you want to try to find it, tell me, "It's too late." I replied, "It's too late not to."

It is impossible to go back in time and do things differently, but it is not too late to look back at the past, realize what went wrong, and then create a better path for the future. We have eyes in the front of our heads for a reason. God wants us moving forward. We are supposed to look back as well, but if we were intended to focus that much on the past, we would have eyes in the back of our heads too, and we clearly do not. My advice was that the past is over, but that doesn't necessarily dictate what's to come. However, what we do today most definitely puts the wheels in motion for our future.

I teach an economics class at a high school in New York, and I routinely tell the students that they must economically prepare for the future according to a ten and twenty year rule. In other words, how they spend money today, dictates how they live in the next ten and twenty tears. If I live it up in my thirties, I will have very little to show for it in my forties and fifties. On the other hand, if I save in my forties and fifties, I will be ready for my sixties and seventies. The same holds true for health.

In this man's case, he has every reason to begin a solid health regiment. A moderate exercise program can go a long way towards better health. I continued on by telling him that the chosen lifestyle of his fifties would dictate the quality of life in his sixties. It was not too late for him at all, and it's not too late for you either. I have another acquaintance who also asked for advice. He too was overweight, lived a very sedentary lifestyle, and had just suffered a mild heart attack. As I was writing this very essay, I originally wrote that, "He most unfortunately suffered a mild heart attack." But the truth is, it wasn't unfortunate. In fact, the heart attack probably saved his life. In a perfect world, he would have been doing all of the right things and this never would have come to pass. However, this isn't a perfect world. You should see him now. He works out daily, has lost somewhere in the neighborhood of fifty pounds, and has now attained the normal vital signs of blood pressure and pulse rate. It is a great success story, and it came to pass because he made up his mind that it was not too late to make those life saving choices.

This applies to other areas of life too. If you have a calling to make a career change, start looking into it. Remember, and you may have heard this said before by someone else, "The grass isn't always greener on the other side; it is greener wherever you decide to water it." That stated, be cautious when making major decisions. Consider all of the options first, and avoid reactions. Follow the same strategy with your health too. See your doctor and develop an appropriate plan that is right for you. Do not pay attention to what others around you are doing. They aren't you, and they do not have the same struggles, limitations, strengths, or weaknesses. You are a unique individual and therefore need a unique plan of action. Your future is being built right now as we speak. What you are doing today directly affects how you will live ten years from now.

This being the case, I have two fundamentally important questions for you to answer, and I hope that they will help to guide your decisions today, as well as tomorrow. First, where do you want to be ten years from now? Will you be heading into retirement, or is this a time where you will be at the peak of your income range? The second question is one that most overlook. Where you want to be is one thing, but how you want to be in ten years is quite another. This question helped me to decide to retire from competitive powerlifting. As I head into my late forties, I have a vision of how I want to look and feel in my late fifties, and hobbling around with a cane, or worse, doesn't fit in with my mind's picture. That doesn't mean, if I am able, that I won't step out of retirement from time to time to set a new world record. But it does mean that I recognize that the day to day pounding of heavy benching, squatting, and deadlifting is no longer for me. It's a piece of the puzzle that no longer fits, and that's all right. Life without adaptation is death, and there are other avenues waiting. They wait for us all, so don't be discouraged if you are facing changes. It's often been said that when one door closes another opens, but it is true. Changes sometimes bring pain, but it's a necessary part of our growth, so don't shy away from it. Look to your future, but live day by day, capitalizing on every opportunity. If you can read this, you probably have the necessary means to re-route the course of your life's path. It's too late not to!

Affirmations:

1) Today, regardless of age, I will begin creating a vision for what I want to become.
2) Today I will create a new and better path for my life and start living according to the championship vision that I have of myself.
3) From this point on, I am determined and destined for victory!

CHAPTER 19

What You Don't Do Makes You Great!

My Family! They have a great future ahead and so do you.
Doing what's right and straightforward while choosing to
resist temptation always sets you up for victory later!

Earlier today I was driving my children to a local hospital where one of them volunteers. The youngest being only ten is not yet eligible to do so, but when he reaches the age of fourteen, like his brother, he will. As we were driving, I took stock of my great fortune in life and told my two boys how blessed I was to have them. I told them that they were the greatest and how proud I was of their accomplishments. My fourteen year-old, named Ethan, looked at me and asked, "Why are you so proud of us? It's not like we've done anything great." I really didn't have to think of or rehearse my response, because I have been trying to live according to this philosophy for most of my life. I truly believe that champions can come in many different forms, and they are not limited to those who win gold medals or who wear large diamond rings, or whose names are screamed by adoring people sitting in the audience.

In the cases of my children, Trent's two boys, as well as the many others out there, they are champions, but not necessarily because of what they did. It's also about what they don't do! I went on to explain to Ethan and Sam that they are leaders and role models because of who they are and not because of what they are, and that is really what a champion should be all about. In every sense of the word, champions should be pointers of a way, guiding people toward the right paths to take in life, and away from those that lead to a downward spiraling of the self. Champions should be leading by example, and that means doing the right things at the right time, and that also means having the stalwartness and value-based commitments to resist the power of temptation. To be able to recognize the bad roads of life and steer clear of them requires a special strength, and even some world champion athletes fail to possess it. I told my two boys that they should be incredibly proud of the way that they have lived their lives thus far. They don't drink alcohol or smoke or steal my prescription drugs from the closet. Neither of them go to places on the Internet that violate the ethics of our household, or, more importantly, our commitments as Christians and members of a greater society. They don't bully other children, especially those who are most vulnerable to this type of cowardly behavior. They don't attack people from behind the security of a computer screen on Facebook or Twitter. They don't lie to their mother or me, even when they know they have done wrong, and I could continue on, but I'm sure that I have driven the point home. On top of that, they both engage in community service and volunteer for different organizations, all while maintaining Honor Roll status at school for their high grades. And I can tell you that those scores on the report card don't come easily. They have to work for them.

When you add up all of the beneficial things that truly successful people do and all of the harmful things that they don't do, you have a formula for success. I have met and spent time with a lot of people, many of them the best in their athletic endeavors, but I would consider only a handful of them to be what I would define as reliable and/or dependable in the bigger picture of life. I'm not being critical here, but just because a man or woman is able to beat others at a game does not mean that this qualifies him or her as a champion at living. As far as I am concerned, there is much more that needs to be done outside the world of sports to earn this prestigious title. As I stated earlier, there are many ways that people can become champions, and living a service oriented and minded life is one of those ways, but it isn't easy, and you will have to stand the test if time. Doing what is right also implies that we are not doing what is wrong, and remember, we will only be as strong as the weakest link in the chain of our respective lives, so strengthen those areas. The rewards of this philosophy are potentially great though, so keep on course, and don't ever let those going down drag you with them. Living a value-based and driven life always puts you in a position to succeed later, and not everyone can say that. Think of the number of times you have seen people with great potential, seemingly on a journey to the top, derail themselves with one or two terrible and life altering choices. I thank God and the Lord above every day for the things that my children both decide to do and decide not to do. Life can be brutally tough and loaded with destiny killing temptations, and that is why I think that those who are able to negotiate through those proverbial mine fields deserve a special respect.

I don't want you leaving this chapter with the wrong impression however. Everyone one of us fails, and we all make mistakes. Other than the Lord Jesus, no one is perfect, and neither are my children. I expect them to fall from time to time, but I also expect them to get back up, and I want the same for you. Regardless of where you presently are in life, you can regroup, alter your course, and start again. I know that you can, because I have seen people succeed after some of the biggest fails possible.

They overcame, and so can you! If you are already on the course for victory, stay true. Somewhat ironically and either way, this chapter is just as much about the future as it is about the present. Look where you want to be tomorrow, and then a week from now, and then a month, and so on, and move in that direction forever more. Remember, being a champion is not just about what you are going to do; it's also about what you aren't going to do, because that's where your journey will inevitably begin!

Affirmations:

1) I will resist temptation, because doing what's right today sets me up for victory tomorrow.
2) Today I will recognize the inherent bravery and courage of not joining in on negative and/or life-changing activities.
3) Today I will be the one that provides help to someone being bullied.

CHAPTER 20

The Value of Nutrition

Being a guest speaker takes a lot of preparation. In this photo,
I am speaking on the subject of proper nutrition.

Being an athlete who has always relied on intense training as my main source for staying healthy and keeping my weight down, I never really understood the importance of proper nutrition, until now. Since the start of my journey to better health and wellness on the ranch of the "Biggest

Loser," I found that I needed to continue my quest for deeper knowledge and understanding of nutrition. To do this I became a certified nutrition coach. This was important to me because the nutritional piece has always been the missing link for me. Equally as important to me was the ability to share good and solid information. With so much overwhelming and (oftentimes misleading) information out there, it is no wonder we are all confused about nutrition, eating healthfully and living a healthy lifestyle. I now know that exercise alone is not enough, especially as we get older and find ourselves with more responsibility and less time to dedicate to working out. Proper nutrition is just as important to your health and wellness as exercise. I have come to realize that it is not just about losing pounds, as our society would have us believe but, it's about feeling good, sleeping well, maintaining hormonal balance in the body, and stabilizing blood sugar.

I now believe in working towards living a holistic and balanced lifestyle. Finding balance in your life can be very challenging. It has to be looked at as a lifelong commitment. Without balance, things can get out of sync internally as well as externally, leading to many of the health issues we are faced with today. Therefore, new life long healthy habits must be developed. Because we are all creatures of habit, this process will undoubtedly require time, commitment, and consistency.

Here are (4) strategies for eating to stabilize your blood sugar and maintain hormonal balance in your body:

1. **Eat breakfast every morning! (You should eat within one hour of waking up).** Starting your day off with a solid breakfast is a great way to boost your metabolism and fuel your body with macronutrients. Giving your body protein, carbohydrates, and fats with every meal will help keep it from converting your lean muscle for energy. Proteins will help with building and maintaining muscle as well as recovery. Carbohydrates are converted to glucose which is used for energy. Healthy fats, monounsaturated fats, polyunsaturated fats, and omega play a huge role in helping you manage your moods, fight fatigue, and stay full. As your stomach empties, carbohydrates are broken down first. This is why when you eat a meal that is composed entirely of carbohydrates you feel

hungry a short time after. After carbs are broken down, proteins follow (they take longer to break down). Finally, your body breaks down fats. Fats take the longest.

2. **Eat every 3 hours from the time you eat breakfast.** This is important for stabilizing your blood sugar and creating homeostasis in your body. Every time you overeat, skip a meal, or don't eat at all, you send your body into an unbalanced state, causing it to release and sometimes over release hormones to get your body back to that balanced state. This done over and over again will put you on track for many of the diseases that have become more and more common in our society.

3. **Be sure <u>NOT</u> to go any longer than <u>4 HOURS without eating!!!!!</u>** When you do, your body goes into survival mode and stores fat. Eating regularly (protein, carbs and fats) throughout the day will boost your metabolism and provide you with the energy needed to push through the day.

4. **Eat real food.** The body knows exactly what to do with real food but isn't so sure of what to do with highly processed items (I won't call it food). Processed items lack any nutritional value. Fruits and vegetable growing from the earth will provide us with all nutrients and vitamins needed to maintain health and wellness.

Affirmations:

1) Today I will recognize the power of good nutrition and choose accordingly.
2) Today I will use portion control.
3) Today I will choose to avoid those foods that I know pull me away from being my best.

CHAPTER 21

Training for Life

I went on the Biggest Loser because of my family.

I created the "Training for Life System" as a result of being on NBC's hit reality show, "The Biggest Loser." On the ranch, I was able to rekindle my passion for training and learn some valuable information that would force me to reprogram my thought process. I have to admit it was truly the jumpstart I needed to get back on track. You see, I will be the first to admit that I was not prepared for life after sports. By not understanding or changing my over indulgent eating habits that I developed as a top level athlete, I ended up at 445 lbs. When my playing days were over, I felt as though I had nothing else to train for. I had no real motivation. I knew that when my time was up on the ranch, I would need to put some things in place to help keep me going and motivated on my journey. My initial motivation for going on the show was to get healthy so that I could to be around for my wife and kids. I'm an athlete and have been one my entire life. Finally, I feel as though I have gotten my "athlete back." For many years I let life get in the way of me taking care of me. I worked long hours, overate, and found myself always doing for others first, putting myself at the bottom of totem pole. Fortunately, I was able to get myself back on track and did so with the sole purpose of living a healthier life for me and my family. I felt that by creating a system that gives you a real reason to train and eat right I could help motivate other people to choose a healthier lifestyle as well. I realized there had to be other people out there just like me who needed a jumpstart, a few words of encouragement, and a blueprint for becoming healthier.

The Training for Life System is about conditioning your mind, body, and soul for a healthy, long, functional life, full of happiness and joy. We are undoubtedly, happier individuals when we feel good about ourselves. When we look in the mirror and are happy with whom and what we see. Are you happy with what you see? Only you can answer that question. I know what it's like to struggle with weight and not feel good because of the extra weight I was carrying. I know what it's like when your joints ache and hurt and when things don't quite fit anymore. I know what it's like to let yourself go to a place that is unhealthy both physically and mentally and wonder how in the world you got there. Well… it's time to take back control of your life!

Here are (4) areas of focus for "Training For Life":

1. **Your mindset** - Have a plan for dealing with the ups and the downs. Things are going to happen that can and will side-track you. How many times have you started something and are doing very well with it and then all of a sudden, something happens and you find yourself off track, wondering what happened? You have to think ahead and plan for that time. Remember, this is about the rest of your life!

2. **Make a holistic lifestyle shift-** This is the only real way to build those healthy habits needed to maintain a healthy lifestyle. That shift includes focusing on:
   - Sleep habits / rest & recovery
   - Nutrition
   - Exercise
   - Stress management
   - Positive relationships

3. **Use my incorporation plan-** In my Training For Life System I like to focus on incorporating more vegetables and fruits into your day instead of focusing on of all the things you cannot eat. Focus on eating more servings of fruits and vegetables. Drink more water and eat smaller servings of lean proteins (3 to 4oz for women and 4 to 5 oz for men) per meal if you are a meat eater.

4. **You must work the process of living healthy**… and let weight loss be the byproduct of that process. I believe we must reprogram ourselves from what we have been taught is important when it comes to being healthy and that's the number on the dreaded **"scale."** There are other factors that go into determining your health and wellness.

My advice is to never give up! Commit to self and "Train For Life."

Affirmations:

1) Today I will jump start my life, energize, and recommit to a better and healthier me.
2) Today I will focus my energies on those things that truly matter and not on the images that the media portray as "worthy."
3) Today I will begin to change my lifestyle habits and better every area of my being.

My family continues to inspire me to even better health.

CHAPTER 22

Understanding the Process

Playing in the Sugar Bowl for the national
championship (vs. the University of Miami)

There is a process for everything we do in life. In order to affect any
changes, you will have to examine the way that you do what you do. One
thing is for sure; that area of your life giving you trouble isn't going to fix
itself. According to Google, the word "process" is defined as "a series of

steps or actions taken in order to achieve a particular end." So what does that mean? What we do or don't do on a daily basis is a part of our own individual process. I believe there is a process for winning and losing, being positive or negative, living healthfully or unhealthfully. If I said I wanted to win a state championship, national championship or even a world championship, I would first have to figure out the best way to go about it. If I am either unable to decode the process for making it happen, or just as importantly, if I do not commit to executing it on a daily basis, it will never happen! Figuring out the solution to the problem is hard enough, but once you've figured that winning formula out, it must be executed on every level and at every facet! People often talk about what goals they want to achieve, but considering the process attached to it is almost never discussed. You must study what winners do and champions do. How do they think? How do they prepare both mentally and physically for success? When we can understand the process, we can make the necessary changes to achieve great things!

During my football days at the University of Alabama, a process was included in nearly everything that my teammates and I did. Fortunately, many of those things have stayed with us well after our playing days at the Capstone. At the root, the processes at Alabama were about winning, about becoming champions. We were taught to "do the little things right every day," and, if we did, the bigger things would be taken care of. We were taught to work hard every day and not let one day go by without a focused concentration on getting better. One of the many underlining messages passed on to us was "Nothing ever stays the same! We either get better or we get worse!" So, you have to make a decision. Which is it going to be? If you choose getting better, and I hope you do, you are going to have to work to make it happen.

In terms of the process at the University of Alabama, it was quite intense. Every week we would review game films, and the coaches would grade our performances, and there was a system to that too. Since I was an offensive lineman, our line coach would watch me either the evening of or day after the game on film and then grade me. Again, he did this for every single play. If there were seventy snaps of the ball, I would get seventy grades. They would then be averaged into a final score. You can get a feel for how difficult coaching would be at that level of football as well because he had to do that for every player on the line, and he looked for the smallest of details too. If I didn't get off the ball fast enough and my shoulder turned, I would likely receive a negative score for that play. Those are the kinds of small details that the coaches are looking at because it's the small things that make the great things possible. I averaged in the high eighties, so my scores were always strong, but that's because I had a system too.

To participate at that level one has to learn very quickly. The Southeastern Conference is known for its high level of competition, so if you are going to play in it, you will have to be both mentally and physically tough, unselfish, and dedicated (to excellence with every single play). You have to have a willingness to compete. The work ethic needed to play G.A.T.A football has crossed over into the other areas of my life as well, and I am grateful to have shared all that I did with my "Bama brothers," both past and present. Donning the crimson and white was truly and honor and a dream come true. In large part, the dream came true because of the process that I implemented. Just like the process of playing a game and being an athlete, there is a process for success in anything. Develop your plan today, and start running after your dreams.

Affirmations:

1) I will start to develop a systematic plan for success.
2) I will begin to chase my dreams by implementing my plan.
3) I will enjoy doing the small things well, because without them, the big things won't happen.

CHAPTER 23

What's Next?

Because Trent and I believe that our experiences could be beneficial to you or someone you know, we thought it would be appropriate to take you on a written tour of the respective journeys of our lives. We began by commenting on our youthful days as up-and-comers, then moved to an era when we were at the crests of our athletic endeavors, and finally to our current location on the path of life. Again though, please do not mistake this book for a biography of any kind. We're not the focus of importance; you are, and that is why we thought that we should share some of our lessons learned! At the core, we felt that our journeys could help to move you on yours, and we hope and pray that you found our intuitions to be correct. To do otherwise is to fall short of the targeted outcome, and neither of us would be satisfied with anything other than the best, so for all of our sakes, please start climbing up the mountain of victory right now.

We further believe that God is never done with his people and that there is always another stage or chapter in the story of life. Writing a book would never have been possible during the peaks of our athletic careers, but stepping away from the competitive arena has granted us more time to do different things. Although he still coaches, Trent has totally retired from playing football, and I only occasionally come out of this more relaxed state when the breaking of a world record entices me to do so. But as I approach the age of 50, it's becoming clearer that one day soon I will no longer have the capabilities to do so, and that's okay. Being retired doesn't mean that we have fewer gifts and talents to develop, it just means that we have different gifts and talents to develop; and that concept holds true for every single man and woman.

We don't know where you are in your book of life, but we are 100% convinced that it can turn out to be a great one. As such, we would like to share one final thought as we head to a close in our travels together. I allowed one of my friends to read a couple of chapters of this book, and his response was one of surprise. He put the papers down and then said with a smile, "Bill, I had no idea you were such a talented writer." To what extent I am in possession of this gift is irrelevant. I always wanted to write, but I never had the time. Now that the athletic door in the voyage of my life is quickly closing, another one has opened to take its place. My friend's comment made me wonder how many other things we might be able to do, and the same is true for you. In that sense, all of us have a virtually infinite amount of talent to work with and "perfect." Regardless of your present situation, you can become that person that you once thought about becoming, but you might have to alter the way that you do it. The more you as a person changes, the greater the likelihood that your dreams will have to as well, and that's all right. That process is part of the game and journey that we call life, and without change, life ends, so don't be afraid of it. Instead, look for the opportunities that have attached themselves to those fluctuations that are sure to come. It is there that the success of your future can be found.

As for us, we plan on developing a project called the Youth Wellness Academy. We just recently began teaching a personal security and self-defense course, and we continue to motivationally speak when those opportunities are presented. Additionally, we have a number of other things that we are giving thought to, including a second book. It's now time to head to the next stage of the journey, and we know it's going to be incredible…for all of us!

God bless, be happy, and live with love, strength, and courage!

Bill and Trent

ABOUT THE AUTHOR

BILL CLARK is a former Olympic Weightlifter and World Champion Powerlifter. Bill has set over 140 world records in both Powerlifting and strongman events; including a 400 plus pound one-handed deadlift (weighing under 200 pounds). Bill is a motivational speaker and often times rolls up frying pans, bends steel bars and wrenches, and tears full decks of playing cards during his presentations. Bill has been featured on TV and in numbers of newspapers and magazines and loves to spread the message that "Everyone can be great." Bill is a certified Strength Coach and co-teaches a personal security course with his friend and co-author Trent Patterson. Bill Clark also teaches economics and a college-level psychology course at a high school in the Binghamton, NY area.

TRENT PATTERSON played football for the University Of Alabama and was a 3 year starter and a 4 year letterman. Trent, while playing for Alabama, was also voted "lifter of the year" and was a contestant on the TV show The Biggest Loser. Trent is a certified strength and conditioning specialist certified by the National Strength and Conditioning Association. He is a certified nutrition coach certified by Venice Nutrition. He is the creator of Training For Life Systems; a complete training system designed to change the mind, body & soul. He currently coaches high school football, trains athletes to improve performance, and adults to train for life. He and Bill also facilitate a personal safety awareness and prevention (PSAP) course.